*Helga Fritzsche*

# Hamsters

Golden Hamsters, Dwarf Hamsters, Gerbils

Everything about Acquisition, Care,
Nutrition, and Diseases

*Translated by* Arthur Freud and Paul Ugarte
*Edited by* Helgard Niewisch, D.V.M.

With Color Photographs by Outstanding
Animal Photographers
and Drawings by Fritz W. Köhler

## Barron's
Woodbury, New York • London • Toronto • Sydney

First English language edition published in
1982 by Barron's Educational Series, Inc.
© 1980 by Gräfe and Unzer GmbH, Munich,
    West Germany
The title of the German edition is *Hamster*.

All inquiries should be addressed to:
Barron's Educational Series, Inc.
113 Crossways Park Drive
Woodbury, New York 11797


Library of Congress Catalog Card No. 82-1712
International Standard Book No. 0-8120-2422-2

**Library of Congress Cataloging in Publication Data**

Fritzsche, Helga.
  Hamsters: golden hamsters, dwarf hamsters,
  gerbils.

  Translation of: Hamster.
  Bibliography: p. 69
  Includes index.
  1. Hamsters as pets.     2. Gerbils as pets.
  I. Title.
SF459.H3F7413        636'.93233      82-1712
ISBN 0-8120-2422-2                   AACR2

Front cover: Angora-golden hamster
Inside front cover: Golden hamster with
    stuffed cheek pouches
Inside back cover: Young golden hamster
Back cover (above): Golden hamster and
    long-haired golden hamsters
    (below): Gerbils and young field hamster

*Photographs*
Animal/Thompson: p. 28, upper left, lower left,
    lower right.
Bielfeld: p. 27.
Coleman/Burton: inside front cover; back cover,
    upper left, upper right, lower left; p. 10; p. 28,
    upper right; p. 63.
Limbrunner: back cover, lower right.
Reinhard: inside back cover; pp. 45, 46.
Schmidecker: front cover; p. 9.
Wothe: p. 64.

PRINTED IN HONG KONG
789   490   98

# Contents

# A Word Up Front

When I saw golden hamsters for the first time, nearly 30 years ago, I found their combination of gentle temperament and bearlike clumsiness so amusing that I immediately gave my working sister a full-grown male for her birthday.

Although Butch was not entirely tame, we loved him dearly. He had every possible freedom, and he exploited it richly to our great joy. He seemed to fare extremely well.

Since then I know that golden hamsters can be ideal house companions for working people who would like to have an animal around but who have time only in the evening. This is true even if they live without a garden or a large house. Konrad Lorenz says it well: "I believe that dear God created the golden hamster expressly for the poor animal lovers in the big city."

Even children instinctively enjoy an amusing, softly clad, little hamster. They need only learn that they must show him consideration, that he needs his rest during the day and they can occupy themselves with him only in the evening, and that he is not a toy even though he seems like one.

Golden hamsters do not have a long history as domestic animals. Nonetheless, they have become familiar pets, and through selection and breeding they have become thoroughly domesticated in a variety of colors.

This distinguishes them from the closely related dwarf hamsters, which have been with us for only a few years. They are less well known and not common in stores. They are hardly domesticated and resemble the members of their species that live in the open. But even they, like golden hamsters, can be tamed to eat out of your hand. By the way, the often used expression "easy to care for" in connection with golden hamsters and dwarf hamsters is incorrect, even if these animals are less work than a dog or cat.

With this book I would like to help you to understand your hamster and to care for him in a fitting manner, in order that the animal may live comfortably with you and that you may enjoy him.

At the end of this book you will find a special chapter about gerbils (Mongolian desert mice). It was written because these hamster-related creatures are being offered more and more in pet shops and because up to now little useful information about their nature and care has been available to prospective owners. Because of some differences they cannot be dealt with in common with hamsters.

In closing I would like to heartily thank all those who helped me with their expert advice and by supplying me with pertinent literature: hamster and gerbil owners of long standing, Professor and Doctor of Veterinary Medicine G. Wachendörfer, and especially zoologists Professor Dr. Jochen Niethammer and Miss Ute Hamann. I likewise express my thanks to the photographers who provided the color photographs and to Mr. Fritz W. Köhler, who prepared the drawings.

Helga Fritzsche

# Choosing a Hamster

## Is a Hamster Right for You?

This question should be resolved as promptly as possible and only after you have considered the following points.

- A hamster requires some work. He needs fresh food and water daily; his cage must be cleaned at least once a week, and the bedding must be changed. Specifically, in the area where he urinates the bedding must be changed every 2 or 3 days so the animal will feel comfortable.
- Hamsters often nip. This is most common in the beginning when they are frightened or are disturbed in their sleep. For this reason you must have lots of patience and learn to adjust to the animals.

Figure 1 *The hamster is active at night; as a rule it sleeps all day.*

- Hamsters require more than just a minimum of freedom of movement; therefore as large a cage as possible should be provided. Since this is a one-time acquisition, a somewhat higher price should not deter you.
- The hamster will stay healthy and reach his maximum age of 2–4 years only if

he is permitted to sleep undisturbed during the day (Figure 1). Consequently, the cage should be situated in a quiet location. It is also up to you to make it clear to your children that they must be considerate and allow the animal to rest, even if he comes out of the nest during the day with half-closed eyes in order to nibble a little food. Nothing more than a gentle stroking should be permitted at such times. The hamster's active period begins only in the evening, in keeping with these animals' way of life in the wild.

- A hamster becomes and remains tame only if you fuss with him each evening. After settling down and becoming adjusted the hamster should be allowed to run around outside the cage at set times and under supervision.
- Can you imagine yourself being required to take an evening trip because the hamster is sick and must be brought to the veterinarian?
- Have you taken into consideration the fact that, as soon as you own a hamster, you must plan your vacation not only for yourself but also for your new companion? Also, that you can't take a vacation if a female hamster is pregnant or has young?

It goes without saying that you are not the type of person who, in order not to be "inconvenienced," would get rid of your animal or have him put to sleep.

- Finally, a pregnant woman should take special care in regard to exposure to hamsters and other rodents, because of a disease called LCM. For detailed information see p. 36.

# Choosing a Hamster

## What Kinds of Hamsters Are There?

Today, the word "hamster" usually calls to mind the golden hamster with gold-colored fur and big black, button eyes. According to zoologists, this species is called *Mesocricetus auratus* and comes from Syria.

The unfortunately rare, indigenous golden hamster or field hamster *(Cricetus cricetus)* is familiar to only a few individuals. For the most part he is known only from pictures. This large (often 10 inches long), strong, and more aggressive animal is, of course, unsuited to be a pet.

In addition to large hamsters and the medium-sized or "middle hamsters" (as one could also call the golden hamster), there is a group of dwarf hamsters, of which two kinds are being found in increasing numbers in pet shops: the Chinese (striped) hamster *(Cricetulus griseus)* and the Djungarian or striped hairy-footed dwarf hamster

*(Phodopus sungorus)*. They have their origins in Asia: North China, Siberia, and Mongolia.

Hamsters belong to the rodents (zoologically Rodentia). They all have especially pretty and attractively patterned fur.

Anatomical characteristics are rooted molar teeth, cheek pouches in which provisions can be carried, and a bichambered stomach.

A special advantage is that hamsters which are maintained in a clean fashion do not emit an unpleasant odor, as tame rats and mice do.

## Which Hamster Types Are Available to Choose From?

Whether you select a golden hamster or a dwarf hamster is a matter of taste. The demands of care and feeding are similar, and either animal will become tame if properly treated.

Figure 2 *Hamster types with a comparison of size from left to right: field hamster, golden hamster, Chinese dwarf hamster, striped hairy-footed dwarf hamster.*

Plate 1  *Golden hamster couple (Angora).*

The space reqirements for the various types are, despite the differences in size, about the same. Since the dwarf hamster should run around the room less than the golden hamster because of his small size (danger of a mishap from being overlooked!), abundant freedom of movement in the cage is especially important.

**Golden hamsters** are so well known that I need not describe them here. There are also relatively new strains with "Teddy bear fur" or Angora-like coats (Plate 1) and also genuine albinos (previously there were only "Russian hamsters," white with dark stripes), and golden hamsters with bluish fur or less pretty ones with pug heads.

**Chinese (striped) hamsters** (Plate 2) become only as big as half-grown golden hamsters. Young animals have gray fur; older ones, more brownish, thick, soft fur. The tail is longer than the foot; the soles are almost hairless. Young animals tame easily; older ones, only very rarely.

**Striped hairy-footed (Djungarian) dwarf hamsters** (Plate 2) in a summer coat have a gray-brown face; the upper head and the ears are dark brown, almost black. The fur is clear around the lips, above the eyes, and behind the ears. A brownish black central stripe runs from the head (becoming wider in the shoulder area) and over the back. On each side the animal has four "indentations" in the direction of the belly. The belly is white furred, and the thick little hind feet are densely covered with fur, even along the soles—hence the name "hairy-footed." The little tail is extremely short. The animals are better natured than the more familiar striped hamsters. In the first winter of their lives nearly all striped hairy-footed dwarfs acquire a brighter coat earlier and keep it longer if they are not kept in too warm a place (68°F).

Up to now there have been only Chinese and striped hairy-footed dwarf hamsters in the original colors. Through deliberate selection and cross-breeding of golden hamsters a few new breeding types have become available. I want to say something here about the appearance and characteristics of these animals, so that the choice will be easier for you.

**Fawn-colored golden hamsters** with smooth, short, gold-colored fur live the longest and are the most vivacious.

**Dappled hamsters** with smooth fur, in which light beige alternates with dark brown, are pretty but nervous and timid, and need an especially sensitive, calm guardian. They are more susceptible to infectious diseases than the others and have a relatively shorter life expectancy.

**Russian hamsters** and **albinos** are valued as being especially tame; like the **beige-colored golden hamsters,** they encounter the fewest problems in breeding and in rearing their young. Russian hamsters, like Russian rabbits, have no pure white fur, but rather darker markings on the tail and ears. Albinos are pure white with red eyes.

**Teddy** or **Angora hamsters** have a velour-like coat (females) or longer, silkier fur (males). These animals are less robust than the breeds with short, smooth coats.

8

# Considerations before Purchasing

Of course, you'd like to buy a young, healthy hamster. For this reason observe the animals in the pet store or at the breeder closely. If possible, do this in the late afternoon when the animals are not in a deep sleep.

At the breeder you may also learn something about the nature of the parents—tame parents, for the most part, have offspring of a similar nature.

### One Hamster, A Pair or A Group?

*Golden hamsters* can be maintained best as single animals. All other things being equal, they feel quite comfortable when kept alone. It makes no difference whether you opt for a male or a female.

Maintaining a pair or several animals is advisable only if you want to breed them. You will find details in the section entitled "Reproduction and Breeding" (p. 38). Maintenance of *one* hamster is much easier!

With *dwarf hamsters,* it is possible to care for two sisters from the same litter together. However, such a pair must not be separated from birth on. If they are separated for even 1 hour and then put back in the cage together, apparently the most important means of recognition, the group odor, is gone. This results in dangerous sessions of biting, and for the most part the animals will no longer adjust to each other.

Even if the sisters are always together, there can be problems, not so much from serious biting as from the fact that the more active, "dominant" animal may begin to threaten the other and to chase her from her feeding and sleeping places. In this way the hounded animal may deteriorate more and more and finally, without any obvious injury or direct starvation, may die from constant stress.

Things need not go this far if you watch your hamsters; a persistent squeak should be cause for alarm. If an animal is visibly thinner, there is nothing left to do but to separate the hostile females. In large cages with more varied and more interesting accoutrements and more possibilities for hiding, there is much less danger of serious conflict.

### Male or Female?

Experienced pet salespersons and breeders can select a male or female for you. However, you may wish to be able to determine sex for your own information. The space between the anus and the genital opening is wide in males, but narrow in females (Figure 3). Male golden hamsters

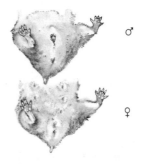

Figure 3 *Differentiation of sex in adult hamsters: The space between the anus and the genital opening is greater in the male (♂) than in the female (♀).*

11

have more pointed buttocks than the rounder and somewhat plumper females of the same type.

In older males the testicles are clearly visible. Older dwarf hamster males have a dark furred area in the abdominal region.

## Age of the Animal at the Time of Purchase

Have the salesperson tell you how old the hamster that you have selected is. From a trustworthy source you can rely on the statement. Three- or four-week-old golden hamsters, which are not yet "lone wolves" but rather mingle with their siblings and play often with them, will adjust much more quickly to you than older animals and will be tamed much faster. This is also true of dwarf hamsters. However, at 3–4 weeks they are in the "flea stage," figuratively speaking. They often hop and run around quite unexpectedly, and they need a calm, confident guardian so that they will not come to any harm or remain timid. An individual who feels unsure of him- or herself had better buy a somewhat larger animal aged 6–7 weeks. Striped hairy-footed dwarf hamsters adapt much better than full-size hamsters to an understanding guardian and can almost always be tamed. The same is not true, however, of Chinese striped hamsters.

## Where to Obtain Your Hamster

There are golden hamsters in pet stores and in the pet departments of department stores almost all year round. If no hamsters are immediately available, you can order an animal and you certainly won't have to wait too long.

If you know a breeder or someone whose golden hamster female has had young ones, he or she will surely be glad to provide you with a young animal as soon as the pup has been weaned. Nowadays, even Chinese striped hamsters are almost always available in the larger pet shops or pet departments. The least plentiful up to now are the especially good-natured striped hairy-footed hamsters. At this time they are not very well known, and they have far fewer offspring than the golden hamster. (Even the Chinese striped hamsters don't multiply as profusely as the golden hamsters.)

If you wish, your pet shop can try to provide you with one or two young dwarf hamsters.

## Expenses of Purchase and Maintenance

At the present time you have to estimate a price of about $3.00 for a golden hamster and about twice that amount for a dwarf hamster. A well-constructed cage that is of adequate size for a single animal will cost from $25 to $40.

Food is cheap: you can feed your golden hamster royally for a whole month for between $2.50 and $3.50.

# Considerations Before Purchasing

## How to Care for It—Where to House It

The hamster house—whether a cage or other container—needs a place that's not too bright and that is protected from drafts. The cage should never be permitted to stand directly in the sun! It should also not stand on the floor, but rather be placed on a table or stand.

The ideal room temperature for golden hamsters is between 68°F and 73°F, which corresponds nicely to the temperature range of the average living room. At temperatures of about 50°F the animals contract a type of winter numbness that is not good for them. Thus always maintain the proper degree of warmth! Animals that are provided with a plentiful supply of shavings and straw can build a circular nest from it and then can tolerate low temperatures of about 60°F.

Dwarf hamsters, which originate in Siberia, are content with much less warmth, especially if they have a warmly padded nest. It is well to note that they do not tolerate high temperatures well (not over 68°F if possible), and on hot days they should be quartered in the coolest room of the house. It should of course be obvious that you cannot maintain dwarf hamsters at Siberian temperatures, because they cannot withdraw into a remote, well-isolated structure as they would in the wild!

Air that is too dry is unhealthy for hamsters, and damp air will also eventually make them sick. A relative humidity that does not exceed 40–50% is ideal. Perhaps you may decide to buy a hygrometer, which shows the exact humidity.

## Checklist: Signs of Health and Disease

You should pay special attention to the following points when selecting your hamster:

• If the hamster that you like most from the standpoint of appearance is awakened, he should come alive quickly, carry his tail high, and show curiosity and enterprise. If he remains apathetic, you'd better not take him.

• The fur of smooth-haired animals should gleam silkily; the fur of Teddy hamsters should look velvety, not shaggy.

• The anus and genital organs should not be smeared with droppings. If they are, the hamster may have diarrhea. Perhaps all the other animals in the cage are also contaminated!

• Heavy and noisy breathing may be indications of disease. Here also there is the danger that the other hamsters may be infected.

• The eyes must be clear and show no traces of any kind of secretion.

# Hamster Equipment

An individual who acquires an animal takes on the responsibility for its well-being. This includes friendly, understanding maintenance as well as proper food and frequent opportunities for the exercise and activity that hamsters naturally require.

## The Hamster Cage

The proper choice of a cage is especially important. You should not hesitate to purchase an adequate one. Cages that are too small or otherwise inadequate are like prison cells for hamsters and are certainly one of the reasons that many animals die prematurely.

There is still no *ideal* hamster cage, only a series of acceptable models as compared to unsatisfactory ones. This is hard to understand since for years golden hamsters have been among the most popular and frequently purchased domestic animals.

As *negative examples* I mention: cages of inadequate size such as 8 inches × 6 inches × 8 inches and with wire mesh running vertically instead of horizontally. Many cages have floors made of wire grating, which, while removable, are of no benefit to the owner, are unpleasant for the hamsters (no chance to burrow!), and can be the cause of behavioral disturbances such as irritability and nipping.

Although no cage can replace or duplicate a natural environment, there are some good models available in pet shops. Being knowledgeable about hamsters will help you to make a better choice.

Our first hamster, Butch, lived in a gigantic wooden box 3 feet long, 2 feet wide, and 20 inches high. This box, which had housed equipment and was thus solidly fashioned, had been heavily modified. Even hamster teeth could not wear down the thick boards, and there was also room enough for running and digging. In addition, in the evening Butch could run and climb continuously for 3 or 4 hours in the living room, if he felt like it. His fireplace climbing escapades between the wall and the cabinet always ended up with him contentedly running around on top of the cabinet, while he gazed down on us from above. When I learned later that this could result in a fatal accident, I decided that such "mountain climbing" was forbidden.

Today nobody keeps hamsters in boxes. The commercially available cages are certainly much easier to clean. A single hamster needs a cage with an area of at least 10 inches × 16 inches × 10 inches in height; the cage should always be made of metal and should have horizontal wire bars since nearly all hamsters like to climb and swing. The distance of the bars from each other should be ½–¾ inch. Even better is the biggest model obtainable at this time with an area of 24 inches × 14 inches and a height of 10 inches, in which your hamster can be at his most active.

I own an even bigger cage, which measures 28 inches × 14 inches in area and 16 inches in height, has horizontal bars, and has a 5-inch-high nest made of sturdy plastic. I can fill this with a thick layer of shavings for digging and building, without having to be afraid that after a while most of it will be lying about the house.

There are similar, sufficiently heavily

# Hamster Equipment

wired cages for small birds, and most of them are suitable for hamsters. Cages manufactured specifically for hamsters have a flatter but, to a certain degree more satisfactory, plastic nest 3 inches in height, while the opening latch on the horizontally barred cage is located above, not on the side, as with a bird cage. This is the better arrangement in the case of babies that are taken out quite frequently.

## Terrarium—Aquarium

A terrarium that is no longer in use for its original purpose can serve as a hamster home, if it is spacious enough. I own an old terrarium 20 inches × 14 inches in area and 13 inches in height, which at the present time is inhabited by a dwarf hamster. The sturdy plastic nest is 4 inches high, the sliding roof and the narrow side are constructed out of fine-meshed wire, and the remaining sides consist of glass. As a substitute for cage bars to climb on, there is an artificial climbing scaffolding made of rods, which must be placed in such a way and fastened so that it cannot fall over.

You can even equip an unused stand aquarium or a complete glass aquarium of sufficient size for your hamster. In narrow aquariums the air circulation is poorer than

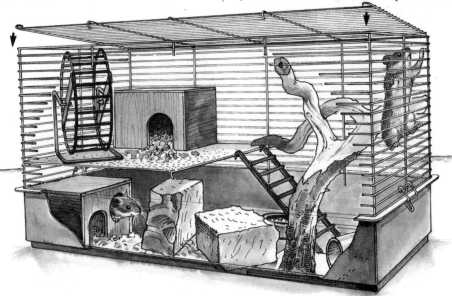

Figure 4 *This is the way a two-story house for a hamster pair may be constructed: a little wood house with an open roof as a home, a hamster wheel for daily exercise in running, a climbing tree (also used for gnawing), bricks (between which interesting openings originate), the proper shavings, and sturdy food and drinking dishes.*

in cages; the animals can become irritable or even sick. Be careful with aquariums that contain adhesives! Silicon pastes that stay soft and rubbery are safe, but silicon pastes that become hard are fatal to animals that gnaw. I know this from personal, painful experience.

Don't forget: terrariums and aquariums need a well-fitting cover, which one can easily make out of galvanized-wire netting. This prevents unexpected escapes, which can end badly for the animals and sadly for the owner.

Also, anyone who has a cat (as I do), which naturally will never comprehend why it is forbidden to catch these attractive and appetizing mice, needs a cover for the hamsters' sake!

### A Box for Digging and Playing

Golden hamsters and Chinese striped hamsters like to dig and burrow, and even hairy-footed ones need opportunities to dig. It is sad to see them deprived of these opportunities. They are accustomed to building burrows and passageways, and this behavior is also true of the domesticated animal. Thus it is ideal for hamsters to have a "digging box" at their disposal outside their cage or other home for use in the evening, which is the time of their greatest activity. Obviously the area and height should not be smaller than the dimensions of the cage—the higher and more spacious the box is, the better. It must be sturdy, somewhat like the aforementioned apparatus box, so that it won't be gnawed through after a short

time, and filled with shavings (see below). Of course even a tall aquarium with a large area (at least 20 inches × 12 inches, preferably more) can serve as a "digging box."

### Proper Bedding

For bedding I recommend, from my own experience, common wood shavings (wood chips, not sawdust!) which are sold in various manufactured forms. They are even recommended in scientific articles, and they are also good for filling the digging box. As for earth, which may occur to you as being more natural, it can transmit disease. If you wish to use earth because of its good burrowing potential, it must be heated beforehand in your oven at 360°F for at least an hour and then cooled for a sufficiently long time.

Sand is not appropriate, and cat litter is best for the urinal section.

The shavings in the hamster home should be changed once a week. Those in the urinal section should be replaced more often, every 2 or 3 days. The digging box needs cleaning only every 3 or 4 days at most.

### The Hamster House and Nesting Material

Every pet shop carries hamster houses in wood or plastic. I have only wooden houses for my animals because even plastic can be gnawed, and I'm afraid that the hamsters could swallow some chips and die. Aside from that, wood is much more "cheerful," and it is not unhygenic, because hamsters do not dirty their nest. If you wish, wooden houses can be ordered from pet stores if they're not in stock.

Simple hamster houses have no floor, a secure (not foldable) roof, and large "window" and "door" areas—consequently two openings. This is especially important when two animals, which often prefer to stay out of each other's way, live together. The customary measurements are 5 inches × 5 inches × 4 inches.

Wooden houses with a floor and a foldable roof are more comfortable. They are especially recommended if a hamster litter is on the way. With these houses it is possible to make quick observations without major disturbance and to see whether everything is in order in the nest. This, of course, is done only when the mother is outside the cage and is busy with a morsel of food.

Amateurs can easily construct wooden houses, even those with foldable roofs. "Duplex houses," which are most popular, consist of pieces of thick wallboard 5–6 inches in length, which you probably can obtain cheaply. Wood pulp can be used as nesting material, as well as unscented facial tissues or straw. If possible, you should peel the wood pulp off in strips. If the layer of shavings is thick enough, a cozy "spherical nest" can be built with the help of the nesting material.

In my experience, hamsters choose the material that they have grown up with if various ones are presented to them. They themselves shape the final design of their home individually. Often the material is pulled into very fine pieces and packed thickly; other times the proffered strips are carried in almost unbroken. The nesting material should be changed about every 4 weeks but not with every cleaning of the cage, as otherwise one would disturb the food storage rooms in the houses too often.

## Play, Amusement, and Exercise

*The Hamster Wheel*

In 1950, when our first hamster came to our house, there were apparently no hamster wheels; at any rate I knew nothing about them, and when I saw one for the first time I was anything but enthusiastic. I thought of wheels driven by slaves for fetching water and grinding wheat. Since

Figure 5

then I've discovered that this thought association is wrong. Most hamsters make full use of their wheels (Figure 5), and of course they do so completely of their own volition. If forced, they would not use them at all. The hamster wheel gives animals that

# Hamsters

are persistent runners in the wild an opportunity for vital exercise without which their muscles would atrophy. It is as necessary for them as cage bars or ladders to climb, digging boxes, and an adequately large cage. This is true even when they are allowed to move about in the house.

There are running wheels made for hamsters in two styles: plastic wheels for hanging on the horizontal rods of the cage (cheaper, shorter lived, and noisier as a result of bumping the cage bars) and metal drums for standing up (more expensive, sturdier, noiseless with a drop of oil and proper placement). The metal drums are adapted to be free standing in aquariums and terrariums. Don't forget to wipe the grease off the wheel compartment!

*A Homemade Device for Fun and Exercise*
In a special article I found a description

Figure 6  *The "carousel ride," with play equipment that you can build yourself, is not only fun but also good exercise for hamsters.*

of a handsome play and exercise device for hamsters that is sold as a kit and that even amateurs can assemble. A round hardwood disk 8–10 inches in diameter is furnished with a bolt in the middle that is fastened to the disk by a washer and nut. You must put the bolt into a thin metal tube, into which it should fit perfectly. The tube is fastened in an approximately 2-inch-thick block of wood about 5 × 3 inches in such a way that the wooden disk is at a slight angle. Since the apparatus needs plenty of space, you make use of it in the room or put it in the cage in the evening for just a while, not as a permanent fixture. It is then always new and interesting for your hamster. Of course this wooden device (see Figure 6) must be kept clean, meaning that from time to time you must wash it with hot water.

*Living Twigs and Branches*
You can offer your hamster a good chance for activity by giving him willow twigs, branches from fruit wood, or other twigs suitable for climbing and gnawing. However, since hamsters' thick hindfeet can easily be caught in the narrow forks of branches, the twigs must be inspected and dangerous sections removed.

*Ornamental Cork as a Building Device*
Every pet shop has ornamental cork. It's really intended for aquariums and terrariums, but I have discovered that hamsters appreciate large pieces of cork and use them as a "finished roof" for a self-constructed underground lair. They like to build every once in a while—golden hamsters and Chinese more, hairy-footed

18

ones somewhat less—and we should give them the opportunity to do so.

Figure 7 *The automatic water bottle is fastened to the cage bars.*

## Food and Water Dishes

Food dishes must be sturdy, easy to clean, and so constructed that they don't tip over. Ceramic or porcelain dishes, which you can get in any pet store, meet these specifications.

For drinking water you had best chose the common, practical, automatic water bottles (Figure 7) that are fastened to the cage bars or are pressed to the glass of aquariums or terrariums with tightly holding rubber suction cups. But please, buy only those with wide necks and metal tops, even if they cost more than other types. They are much easier to clean.

# *Ground Rules for Maintenance and Care*

## Transportation Home and Adjustment

The moment of decision has finally come. It must be this hamster and no other! If you have already purchased some of the hamster's usual food (to make it easier for him to adjust to the change in homes), then the only question now is, Which is the fastest way home? Since transportation means excitement and strain for the little animal, the trip should be kept as brief as possible.

In the store or at the breeder the hamster will be properly packed so that he receives sufficient air and yet cannot escape. Nonetheless, keep the package in sight just for safety's sake. In the car the passenger should hold the box in his or her lap.

Everything at home, it is hoped, is ready for the new arrival: the cage with shavings, house, running wheel, food and water dishes. Otherwise these things must be obtained as quickly as possible.

Place the hamster in his new home, using the proper grip, of course (p. 23). It is a "no-no" to lift him up by the fur or tail because this can hurt and do damage! He'll probably bite, even if you have lifted him according to instructions and have spoken to him in a friendly way, just out of sheer fright and confusion. No wonder—the unfamiliar environment, with its strange odors and noises, frightens him. Also, his previous life, even in a good pet store, was not unqualifiedly suitable to a hamster: exposed to the light, for the most part, without a chance to withdraw because he

was supposed to be seen. If you are afraid of being nipped, you can protect yourself with gloves in the beginning.

Hairy-footed striped dwarf hamsters react to new people and to a new environment primarily by emitting odors from an abdominal gland. These odors are distinctly noticeable, even to our noses, and are more pronounced in males than in females (p. 53). My experience has been that this reaction disappears after a few weeks' adjustment. Nonetheless, it can be rekindled by a new cage or, to cite an example, by a visiting smoker in a house of nonsmokers.

Probably your hamster will withdraw into his house after a brief period of sniffing around. Leave him there completely undisturbed—he will relax all the faster.

Please make it clear to your children that the new house guest cannot be exhibited now or in the near future, because this will frighten him again. He needs time to adjust to his people and to the new home. Thus friends can admire him only after a while and then, of course, only at night. But don't pick him up whatever you do!

With little children, curiosity and the desire to see and feed the hamster during the day are, for the most part, stronger than insight and reason. An acquaintance of mine placed the cage on a wide, sturdy board that her husband had fastened solidly to the wall at so high a level that the children could not reach up to it even from a chair. Now, this is no longer necessary; they respect the slumber periods of their second hamster without such prods to the memory.

# Ground Rules for Maintenance and Care

## Cleaning the Cage

Hamsters are clean animals that groom themselves thoroughly and often and feel comfortable only in a clean cage. Therefore you must without fail change the bedding (shavings) once or twice a week. The hamster should be lodged elsewhere during this activity.

The sleeping quarters, with bedding and paraphernalia, must be aired every 4 weeks, even though normally not dirtied or used as a toilet. Uneaten perishable food (fruit, vegetables, and meat) should be removed daily.

Many times the little holes that hamsters dig to hide in have no floor. In order not to scatter the contents, I use a little trick. I carefully slip a thin board or a plastic scraper underneath and then lift the house. With a little skill it can be put back without the provisions being disturbed.

## Taming: to Feed, to Handle

An animal that takes food from your hand and comes to the wire when its master or mistress appears (instead of hiding) is food-tame or wire-tame.

An animal that listens for his master's or mistress's voice, always enjoys his or her company (even when no food is forthcoming), and likes to be stroked and rubbed gently is completely tame. He meets his owner confidently and has lost all fear. Most hamsters become food-tame after a while if one doesn't handle them roughly. Stroking is much less important to them even when they are fully tame. It means the same to them as mutual grooming, in which animals clean each other. Of course among golden hamsters—which as adult animals are lone wolves, figuratively speaking—this exists only between mother and unweaned children or between sibling pairs that get along well together. With golden hamsters that can be maintained together as pairs (p. 39), and with dwarf pairs that are used to each other, the "conjugal animals" clean each other reciprocally.

Hamsters become finger-tame in many cases. This is more likely to happen if you are calm and patient and play with them every evening. Of course, playtime should begin only when the hamster comes out of his nest of his own accord. No living creature reacts in a friendly manner to being disturbed in its sleep!

For Mickey, a hamster of my acquaintance, the "Taming of the Hamster" went as follows. In the evening, after the little one woke up, cleaned himself thoroughly, and made use of his lavatory section, the family gave him time to eat and drink. Afterwards the mother took him out of the cage (with gloves on) and put him on the table, around which the family sat, all wearing gloves. The hamster ran around, sat up, and ran further. If he came to the edge of the table, he was gently put back, whereby he heard his name each time and a sentence such as: "Look out, Mickey, you'll fall," "No, Mickey, that won't do," "Yes, that's fine, Mickey." Even if he didn't understand what was said, he at least got used to the voices and gradually realized that everyone there was well disposed toward him. It took about 3 months before he stopped nipping, but no one lost patience. Today Mickey is a year old and so tame that he lets himself be carried around, and he climbs on one's lap, on one's sleeve, and on one's pants legs without ever biting. Even strangers have nothing to fear, as I myself can confirm.

There are various ways to make a hamster friendly. But certainly you must spend time with him regularly. There have been animals that right from the start have considered the human hand to be something pleasant (in fact, they permitted themselves to be lifted into the hand). Such hamsters are more friendly and more approachable than others. Please don't take this to mean that you should carry the hamster around as much as possible during his entire waking period, feed him extra morsels (which will cause him to get too fat), and then expect him to jump at your command. Even a perfectly tame hamster needs freedom and sufficient opportunity to occupy himself in a way befitting a hamster: digging, climbing, munching, cleaning himself and, above all, sniffing everything as he runs around the house. This is only right, and it will give you pleasure just to watch him. If you cannot understand this, you should content yourself with stuffed animals.

## Dealing with the Hamster

### Fun or Business?

Strangely enough, articles entitled "Playing with the Hamster" are sometimes found in both good and inferior magazines about golden and dwarf hamsters. The word "playing" is really inappropriate and evokes false impressions.

Thus, children and adults who have had no experience with animals and who do not know that their hamsters must be dealt with on an animal-behavioral basis are encouraged to think of these animals as toys. Thus they play with the little creature, as if he had no feelings of his own, no special needs, and no will of his own. This can cause the hamster to bite. He is then labeled as mean and punished accordingly.

If, moreover, he becomes lethargic, gets sick, and dies relatively young, it only rarely occurs to anyone that treating him

Figure 8 *Stroke the hamster gently with only one finger over his head and back. If he responds with grooming gestures, it is a sign that he likes what you are doing.*

like a toy could be the cause of the problem. Such treatment, however, along with errors in feeding and maintenance, can very well result in death.

Many people will also think longingly of the exuberant games that they know from friendly association with dogs and cats, but

# Ground Rules for Maintenance and Care

the hamster is completely different. You can accustom him to your hand and then stroke him gently (Figure 8) with one finger over his head and back and rub his ears. Having become completely tame, he waddles forward when you call his name, he climbs on your hand and into your lap, and he sits up and "listens" when you talk to him. Many animals climb around and exercise completely of their own volition and with obvious pleasure when they react to a familiar person. Thus they show that they feel safe and at ease with you, and they behave in a completely uninhibited fashion. In this way you really become acquainted with the hamster and understand his individuality. This is real pleasure for you—even without play in our sense of the word!

Hamsters are certainly not to be compared with mammals such as dogs and cats, or even rabbits and guinea pigs, in terms of intelligent behavior—the latter are more adept at learning. Nevertheless, variety is essential in the monotonous environment of a cage, which is a poor substitute for what life in the open offers. Unfortunately there is no possibility of letting the hamster always run free so that he might be able to move and occupy himself in a manner more in keeping with his nature. For this reason the exercise apparatus described on p. 17 is of particular importance.

In addition you should always try to interest the hamster in activity by varying the objects in his cage, such as roots or pieces of bark. In the chapter entitled "Correct Nutrition" (p. 31) you will find a list of well-known, common trees that are nonpoisonous. Of course the branches or twigs should not come directly from trees near a well-traveled automobile road or from plants that have been treated with insecticides or herbicides. Be sure to wash and dry the roots or bits of bark before using them. Then, too, cardboard rolls (uncolored!) from toilet paper are popular for crawling through and gnawing on. Bricks that have been broken in half may be put next to each other so that they won't tip over (1¼–1¾ inches apart for golden hamsters, and 1–1¼ inches apart for dwarf hamsters). Dwarf hamsters not only jump and climb around on them, but also try to crawl through the small crevices. Hard-to-reach crawl spaces, which are very important as refuges from predators when living in the wild, are always interesting to hamsters.

### How to Pick Up a Hamster

If you pick up a hamster by the scruff of the neck, he will generally urinate as a

Figure 9 *A method for lifting: clasp the hamster with one hand in such a way that thumb and fingers enclose his stomach securely. He will not be able to wriggle out of your hand!*

reaction to fright. There is, however, a proper grip as well as various methods for lifting the animal.

*Method 1:* Take the hamster in the palm of your hand and place the other over him so that a warm little pocket results. This is a good way to accustom young animals (even hairy-footed striped dwarfs when they are fully grown) to your hand, even though they may struggle at first. Be sure not to let them escape, as this will only heighten their nervousness. Also an escaping hamster could fall and hurt himself! After a while,

Figure 10 *The "canning technique": Curiosity drives the hamster into a proffered container. When the head and front part are safely secured gently push in the rest of the animal.*

when the little creature is completely calm, gently put him back in the cage.

*Method 2:* Place your hands together in such a way that your fingertips overlap each other and your thumbs are next to each other. Then invert this "roof" over the hamster; as soon as he sits in the trap, close your fingers tightly together.

*Method 3:* Take hold of the hamster with one hand so that your thumb and finger are around his abdomen between his front legs and hindlegs—securely, but loosely and without any pressure (Figure 9).

Each one of these methods requires a quick grip but action without undue haste. If you're too slow, the hamster will escape or you won't be able to catch him at all. Haste is no good either, because it communicates itself and makes animals frightened and aggressive.

Finally, a simple *method for the inexperienced* (known as the "canning technique" (Figure 10) in scientific literature): With one hand you extend a metal box or can to the hamster, for instance, an empty coffee can, in which he will fit well. Most of the time he will scoot headlong into this interesting "cave." As soon as the biting end of the animal is in the container, you can push him completely inside with the other hand. This is an ideal method to suggest to a friendly but inexperienced neighbor who is taking over the care of your hamster during your vacation.

The hamster should never be permitted to remain in the cage while it is being cleaned. During this time put him in a clean, dry 2-gallon pail with straw on the bottom so that the waiting period won't be too unpleasant. He cannot possibly escape from such a container.

## Does He or Doesn't He Bite?

Hamsters bite people if they feel threatened or are frightened—this is not unusual behavior during the first days in

# Ground Rules for Maintenance and Care

new surroundings. With calm, friendly treatment and proper care this type of behavior will soon pass. Punishment or loud scolding is senseless and will only make the by-now completely frightened animal more snappish.

Irritability and snappishness can have different causes: unclean shavings, the wrong food (lack of protein or sometimes a protein excess), disease, and noise. They can also be caused by being picked up too often or by strange people who handle the hamster clumsily. Even a well-adjusted, entirely tame hamster bites "by mistake" if one interferes in his battles with another hamster. This can happen, for example, if a female who is not in the mood is placed in the cage of a male for the purpose of mating, and shows him with her teeth and paws that she wants nothing to do with him. Then you *must* intervene because otherwise the male will be badly roughed up and could even die from his injuries. Don't forget to wear gloves when you intervene!

*Hamsters and Other Domestic Animals*

Hamsters care nothing for the company of other domestic animals and do not adjust to them. I can only advise against attempts in this direction. Every cat will attempt to snatch these "appetizing mice" in its paws. At best it may with great effort control itself in your presence, as it will quickly comprehend that you are not releasing the hamster as some sort of prey.

A very obedient, well-bred dog will probably subdue his hunting urge after one loud "No!" However, I would rather not put this to the test.

Parrots and parakeets do not look upon a hamster as prey. Nonetheless they may peck at him.

My advice is to let the hamster (under supervision) run around only when it is certain that neither cat, dog, nor parrot can get at him. Otherwise you will overtax the patience of the cat and dog, and bring them (even when everything is going well) into a state of tension, which is detrimental. In addition, the cage should always be securely closed and placed in such a way that your other animal(s) cannot claw the bars and knock the cage over.

If you keep other types of rodents (other hamsters, mice, gerbils), always wash your hands with soap before you move from one to the other for feeding or playing. The odor of other rodents excites many hamsters so much that they snap or suddenly attack their cage mate in a fit of fury.

## Running Around in the House

When the hamster is fully grown (6–8 weeks old) and is well adjusted, you can start letting him run around the house in the evening. This should take place in only *one* room, with the doors closed and of course under supervision.

It is better for you if the room has no wallpaper, because all rodents quickly notice when wallpaper has become loose at some point—how they notice it is their secret. The loose piece will be chewed off and dragged away as nesting material. This may seem very funny to some, but it's not everyone's idea of what's amusing.

Plate 3   *Long-haired golden hamster.*

*How You Can Avoid Accidents*

A healthy hamster is extremely curious and active in the evening and at night. If you're not attentive, this can work to his detriment.

- Before the hamster can run loose, all family members must be made aware that no one should carelessly open a door and thereby pinch him behind it, trip over him, or let a dog or cat into the room with unfortunate results.
- Narrow hiding places under furniture have an irresistible attraction for every hamster. He will disappear inside the furniture without fail and perhaps remain hidden so that you are unable to get him out.
- Electric cords should not be accessible. They will definitely be chewed through—annoying for you, highly dangerous for your pet!
- Vases, dishes, and pails filled with water, which the climbing hamster can reach, can be fatal.
- Climbing is certainly fun for the hamster, but be careful that he is not permitted to climb too high up. Even a fall from a height of 3½ feet can be dangerous for him (p. 14). He himself is not capable of judging distances correctly.

*If the Hamster Escapes*

Of course such a thing should not happen at all, because the escapee often comes to a bad end. But if it has happened, what then?

Don't start a wild, noisy pursuit, because a hamster that has become thoroughly frightened is even harder to catch.

Afterwards he will probably be so upset that you'll need plenty of time and patience to make him friendly again. Instead, try with calmness—and a morsel of food. If you don't know where he is, look everywhere that offers possibilities for climbing and hiding. Otherwise the "sunflower seed trick" often helps. This was revealed to me by a friend: You place a particular number of carefully counted sunflower seeds in each room and close the doors. After one night you can easily determine (by the number of sunflower seeds) where the hamster is. You can now lure him out by placing his house or open cage stocked with food on the floor of the room in which you believe him to be. Most of the time he will gladly run into his home of his own accord.

Completely tame animals frequently emerge from hiding even before anyone has noticed that they are missing. Suddenly there they are in, say, the kitchen or the bathroom. They will sit up and, if addressed in a friendly manner, can be picked up without resistance or even with willingness on their part.

If the hamster has escaped outdoors, however, there is little hope of finding him again. Our first hamster escaped and was killed by a cat, which certainly enjoyed the "fat mouse."

Sometimes (although seldom) such an escapee is fortunate. Thus acquaintances on an icy, wintery day found a young hamster in the cellar under an open window. He had tumbled inside there in search of food and warmth. They took him into the house, cared for him, and, since the owner was nowhere to be found, kept the little creature.

Up to now the discussion has focused on danger to the animal. But unsupervised hamsters can cause all kinds of mischief. They chew clothing, newspapers, books, wallpaper, and baseboards in order to fashion a suitable refuge for themselves—which from their point of view is perfectly "legal" behavior but from yours is very annoying!

## Where to Put the Animal While on Vacation

Vacations should be planned—even for the animals that live with us. With good intentions a working solution can be found for all parties concerned.

*Arrangements for One Day*

For 1 day or even (at most!) 2 days you can leave your hamster alone. See that he is well provided with food, fill the drinking dish to the top, and give him an apple or a fresh carrot for juicy food. Remember: The cage should not be in a strong light, in the sun, or right near the radiator. Make sure that during your absence the room temperature (for golden hamsters) does not go over 77°F or below 59°F. For dwarf hamsters do not exceed 74°F.

*Housing for a Longer Time*

If you are going away for several days or perhaps weeks you must choose in advance among the following alternatives:

- Whether the hamster is to be cared for in your house by reliable friends who are knowledgeable about animals.
- Whether he is to be handed over to them to be cared for in their home.
- Whether he is to be accommodated in a pet shop.
- Whether he is to be entrusted to a veterinarian or to an animal hospital.
- Whether he should be taken along on your vacation.

The first two possiblities are almost ideal. And perhaps you *have* dependable friends who understand animals, and who are prepared to take over the care of your pet during vacation time. You could make a reciprocal arrangement!

Choose accommodations in a pet shop only if the owner is favorably known to you and if the cages are not piled up on top of each other during vacation time. If your animal will be well cared for in a shop, you should not object to the price for boarding him, which for the most part is not especially high. I know of one hamster owner who said angrily, "What—so much? For the cost of 4 weeks of care I can buy myself two new hamsters!" and went away. But you obviously do not belong to the category of people who change animals like facial tissues, and you will cheerfully pay accordingly for good care and friendly treatment.

Animal hospitals do not exist everywhere, and besides they are often overcrowded during the summer. By all means, investigate the possibilities for accommodations and guardians before you bring your hamster to a hospital. If you have a good impression, you can register the animal well in advance. Here too, there will, of course, be a fee.

29

# Hamsters

*Pregnant and nursing hamsters* endure environmental change poorly and should continue to be cared for by people familiar to them. Otherwise it is possible that they may eat their young or not suckle them, as a reaction to the stress of transition.

Also, all hamsters should remain in their own familiar cages, as this facilitates the transition. In addition you had better leave instructions indicating which food you normally give and which shavings you use.

*Taking the Hamster with You on Vacation*

If you stay within the country and don't plan too long a trip, you can take the hamster along if suitable quarters are provided.

One or two days before the trip the cage should be cleaned and freshly filled with straw, and the hamster house plentifully supplied with nesting material. Just before the journey fasten the house to the cage floor with glue in such a way that it will not jiggle back and forth. Thus the trip for the hamster will be as comfortable as possible.

Don't ever place the cage where it will get too hot (near the heater, for example), and also watch out that the hamster is not affected by a draft. The ideal thing is for a strapped-in passenger in the back seat to take the cage on his or her lap. If you make a stop, take the hamster (together with his cage) out of the car with you. Even he will probably make use of the pause outside the moving, noisy auto to drink or eat something. At any rate he must have the opportunity to do so. If you have to leave him alone in the car for a short while, make sure that the cage is carefully closed and that the car is not parked in the sun. Also leave the air vents open.

Hamsters are generally unwelcome in motels or inns, even if they stay in their cages and are kept clean.

Your animal stands a better chance of being welcomed in a private home, but you should come to some agreement on this with your host beforehand.

In a vacation apartment you are very much your own boss. Nobody will raise any objection to an orderly and neatly kept hamster; he also cannot cause any trouble if you always keep him in the cage.

Don't forget to take along, for the four-legged vacationer, besides the cage, his wheel, house, food dishes, shavings, and some familiar dry food. If you should be in a small community, it might not be possible to buy these necessities.

In the vacation apartment the hamster will need, just as at home, a place that is quiet during the day, draft-free, and not too brightly lit. Also, in the evening he will require a bit of "entertainment."

*Traveling to a Foreign Country*

Trips to, say, Canada or Mexico often last a long time, as hamsters reckon it, and for this reason they place a considerable burden and strain on the animals. If you intend to take your hamster on such a journey, you had better inquire at the official consulate whether any type of veterinary health certificate or other medical record is necessary for entering the country to which you are going. In this way there will be no unpleasant surprises on the trip.

# Correct Nutrition

Wild golden hamsters and dwarf hamsters feed chiefly on seeds and insects, but they also eat various greens. They are, therefore, omnivores, rather than, as is often assumed, vegetarians. This must be taken into consideration when providing their food, in order to prevent deficiency disease.

## Basic Rules for Feeding

Food and water should be available during the day (even though this is the hamsters' sleeping period). The animals need frequent, small between-meal snacks. Food dishes must be cleaned once a week, and water dishes every other day. The food must be fresh and impeccable in quality. Seeds and pellets that have been stored too long or have become moldy can make the hamster sick. Check the manufacturer's milling date, and store the food in a dry place! Of course, vegetables, fruit, and hay that have spoiled or show molds should not be used.

Greens should not be picked from the edges of highways (because of vehicle exhaust gases), and they should be free of chemical herbicides and pesticides. Store-bought vegetables and fruit must be thoroughly washed with tap water and then completely dried before feeding.

The addition of multivitamins (the kind for small mammals) is highly recommended and especially important during the winter. The drops are either dispensed as prescribed, or the specified dosage for dogs and cats can be appropriately reduced for the body weight of the hamster. Left-over perishable foods such as fruits, vegetables, and, of course, meat are to be removed from the cage daily. In case the animals drag something into the nest (which seldom happens), you must check at least twice weekly to see whether it needs emptying. Otherwise empty the house at greater intervals (p. 21), because hamsters do not at all relish this disruption of their food storage and their home.

Figure 11  *Hamsters can be very stubborn about trying to force precious foods that are too large into their burrows.*

## Dry Food

Dry food is the basic food. There is a compressed food (called pellets) for hamsters that can be given as the only food and that contains all the important nutrients: at least 17.5% protein, 2.5% fat, 58% carbohydrates, 0.3–0.5% calcium, and a maximum of 8.5% crude fiber. Other minerals and necessary vitamins (of which vitamin E is of special importance) are also present in the pellets in appropriate amounts.

Often, unfortunately, the pellets are not readily accepted by the hamsters. (The pellets are sold in large quantities that are undesirable for owners of only one or two hamsters.) Though balanced, the pellet food is monotonous. It doesn't satisfy the hamster's natural desire for variety. For this reason special seed mixes for hamsters are more suitable. The compositions of these vary with the manufacturer, so the best thing is to use the various brands on an alternating basis. From time to time you can offer rolled oats and, more frequently, a peanut or a filbert.

*Dwarf hamsters* are frequently fed golden hamster food. However, they understandably have a preference for smaller seeds. Canary seeds are quite suitable for them. In addition I provide on an alternating basis sunflower seeds, thistle seeds, Moroccan millet, buckwheat, grass seed, linseed, rolled oats, peanuts, and filberts. You can get thistle seed, linseed, buckwheat, and Moroccan millet in seed-specialty shops, if they are not in stock in the pet store.

In addition, both *golden* and *dwarf hamsters* should always have a piece of dog biscuit in the cage, because it contains plenty of protein and minerals and offers sufficient resistance to their constantly growing incisors. It will gradually be chewed up, and then you can replace it with a new one. Even with dog biscuits you should alternate the brands. On occasion I also feed the hamsters a little dry cat food.

## Protein Food

You should regularly offer your hamsters cottage cheese and plain or fruit yogurt. If possible, use a spoon to avoid making a mess. Either one is popular with hamsters and important for their well-being.

My little hamsters now take yogurt and cottage cheese most eagerly, even though they refused them at first. I often place the necessary vitamin drops on top so that everything lands in the hamsters' stomachs instead of in the cage. My male hamster likes to occasionally eat tiny bits of lean, fresh chopped meat; the female, strangely enough, doesn't. I must emphasize here that not even the smallest portion of fresh food should be permitted to remain in the cage because it spoils quickly and may cause disease.

## Live Food

Hamsters also eat insects, as you already know. Perhaps, it is hoped, you are prepared, for the sake of your animal, to overcome a possible aversion to these creatures!

But how does a city person get insects? Even more important, which insects are suitable for food?

*Mealworms*
Every good pet store carries mealworms, that is, beetle larvae. You had best store the larvae in a large, open jam jar half-filled with coarse rolled oats. It should be kept at room temperature, and not near the radiator or in the sun. The "worms" cannot climb up the smooth glass sides of the jar and therefore—important for you—cannot get out. If you provide dried lettuce or other vegetable leaves, which are

# Correct Nutrition

alternated every 2 days, the worms will receive the vitamins that they need. There is absolutely no danger if the larvae turn to pupae and then to their adult stages. The majority of hamsters make no distinction between the stages, as you will see when they eat them.

*Important:* From time to time empty the jar, clean it, dry it, fill it with fresh material, and put the selected mealworms back in it. If this job is put off, mold builds up after a time, and this, if ingested with the mealworms, can make your hamster sick.

### Crickets and Grasshoppers

Many pet shops or specialty breeders of food animals can provide crickets and grasshoppers. Adult hamsters, even dwarf hamsters, are wild about them. But these insects, which are raised at some expense for large reptiles, are relatively costly and are not available everywhere. If you can get

Figure 12 *A variety of food is important. In addition to seeds, insects, and hay, hamsters need greens and dog biscuits.*

them now and then, give two per hamster per day with the normal food ration.

Do not select beetles and other insects from the garden, forest, or field unless you are certain that they have not ingested some kind of insecticide, that they are not protected species, and that the insects you choose will not harm your hamster.

### Flies

I consider flies inappropriate as a food supplement because they *may* transmit diseases to hamsters.

## Fruits, Vegetables, and Other Plant Products ("Moist" Foods)

In addition to a good seed mixture, you should regularly provide a plentiful supply of vegetables and other plant products, as well as (fruit) yogurt, in order to meet the needs of the animal for fluid food contents. It's easy to provide variety with these foods.

• Vegetables that one can buy or grow in the garden (be sure to wash store-bought ones especially well!): carrots, cabbage, endive, cauliflower, broccoli, celery, small green peas and other peas with pods, soft corncobs, cucumbers cut into very thick slices, potatoes (without the leaves and the sprouts, of course), ripe tomatoes, red peppers, and green roots.

• Green foods such as you find when weeding the garden or you can bring home from strolls: dandelions (*Taraxacum officinale*), green grass and shepherd's purse (*Capsella bursa-pastoris*), hogweed (*Heracleum*).

# Hamsters

• Fruits: Apples, either whole or in thick pieces, pears, strawberries, raspberries, plums, bananas, orange slices.

• Herbs and other vitamin-filled foods for the winter: carrots minus the green parts, which are posionous, potatoes without the poisonous seeds and green parts, chicory, radishes, endive, celery, green roots, cucumber slices.

• Fruits in winter: avocado, apples, orange and Mandarin orange slices, bananas.

• In addition, during the entire winter at intervals of 2–3 weeks you can germinate grass, lettuce, and grains in little boxes, keep them moist, put them by the window in the sunlight, and use the young sprouts as food.

• Branches for gnawing: with leaves or (in winter) naked branches from beech trees, maple trees, willow trees, hazelnut trees, fruit trees.

• Types of clover that are especially easy to digest: alfalfa *(Medicago sativa),* hop clover *(Medicago lupulina).*

**The following are poisonous:** raw beans; potato seeds; green parts of potato tubers, carrots, and tomatoes; hemlock *(Conium maculatum);* laburnum *(Laburnum);* meadow saffron *(Colchicum autumnale).*

## Roughage

High-quality hay should always be available in small quantities. It is indispensable as a valued food supplement and as bedding for the nest.

*Important:* Hay must be dry and be stored in a well-ventilated place so that it will not spoil.

## Drinking Water

You should offer water continuously in the automatic drinking bottle mentioned on p. 19. At least twice a week the bottle should be cleaned with hot water and a bottle brush and filled with water that is at room temperature. Strongly chlorinated water is harmful. If necessary, use uncarbonated mineral water.

Experiences with hamsters and water vary. My golden hamster and my dwarf hamsters take no water, although I have repeatedly offered it to them. A very seasoned owner of dwarf hamsters had a completely different experience with her animals: they were irritable and snappish when water was not constantly at their disposal. In both of the above instances the hamsters received abundant amounts of green and other plant foods. Perhaps room temperature and humidity play a role here too. In any event thirst is greater during periods of heat and on hot summer days. If there is any doubt in your mind, it's better to offer drinking water.

## Daily Food Needs of the Adult Animal

| | |
|---|---|
| Golden hamster | about ½ ounce mixed-seed food. |
| Dwarf hamster | about ¼ ounce mixed-seed food. |

In addition, 6–8 mealworms, dog biscuits, hay, and alternating green and "moist" food, supplied in sufficient quantity so that it's not completely eaten. Remove the rest the next day!

Pregnant and nursing female hamsters require somewhat greater amounts.

# When Your Hamster Is Sick

## Prevention Is Better than Treatment

Hamsters that are properly cared for and fed often reach a greater age than the frequently estimated 2 years, and they only seldom become sick. They are more resistant, and disease-causing agents cannot take hold as easily and multiply. According to statements by experienced breeders, milk can sometimes be helpful in fighting fresh infections. However, for stomach and intestinal diseases milk is dangerous and therefore should not be given!

Bacteria, viruses, and parasites can be transmitted to hamsters by other house pets; in certain cases even human diseases pose a danger to these animals. Therefore one should wash his or her hands not only after, but also before, caring for and handling the pets.

## Common Ailments

*Symptoms of Deficiency*

Lack of a varied diet can lead to deficiency syndrome.

Figure 13 *The vitamin drops that your hamster needs regularly, as well as medicine, are ideally given in a spoonful of yogurt—his favorite food.*

Symptoms: The animal loses hair, develops a body rash, and has a dull appearance.

Treatment: Provide high-grade hamster food or change to a varied diet immediately—and your pet will recover quickly.

In advanced cases a veterinarian's help is necessary. Treatment with vitamin drops has proved successful.

In winter green foods, may contain fewer vitamins. Therefore you should give a golden hamster 1 vitamin drop every other day, and a dwarf hamster 1 drop twice a week. If you offer the vitamins with yogurt (Figure 13) or mealworms, you will have a guarantee that your pet will get everything.

*Diarrhea*

Diarrhea can be caused by spoiled, wet, or cold foods, by being too cold or by damp bedding, or by drafts.

Symptoms: The droppings are soft or almost liquid, and smell sour or rotten.

Treatment: Remove "moist" foods. Feed dry rice lightly cooked in water, and offer good hay. For drinking provide lukewarm camomile tea, very thin black tea, or peppermint tea—without sugar, of course!

Hamsters with diarrhea due to overfeeding with corn may be given a dash of charcoal or a small amount of moistened internal (Luvos) earth powder for about 2–3 days to absorb the intestinal fluids.

Bedding and nesting materials must be changed once or twice daily, and food and water dishes cleaned daily with hot water.

If symptoms of diarrhea persist unabated, you should consult a veterinarian. Otherwise the hamster will lose too much weight and will waste away quickly.

# Hamsters

After the animal has recovered, the cage should be washed with hot water and disinfectant.

## Wet Tail

This disease occurs in some hamster breeds. The cause is an intestinal bacterial infection. Improper maintenance conditions (too high temperatures; too much or too little humidity) can encourage this disease. Susceptibility to the condition seems to be enhanced by any stress situations experienced by the hamster.

Symptoms: The hamster's tail and anal area, as well as parts of the belly, are damp or soiled with soft excrement.

Treatment: As with diarrhea, remedy all aspects of maintenance that may be questionable, particularly those that may be considered stressful. Offer alfalfa cubes, oatmeal, always fresh roughage. A veterinarian can prescribe an antibiotic to be given in the drinking water.

## Skin Diseases

Older animals frequently develop areas of hair loss, as well as tumorlike growths, without any impairment of vitality or appetite. They can live a long time with these. Good care and proper nutrition are all that are necessary. These symptoms are not contagious for people.

## Colds and Pneumonia

Hamsters may develop pneumonia from temperatures that are too low or too high, from air that is too dry or too damp, or from drafts.

Symptoms: The hamster is lethargic and stays motionless in a corner of the cage with ruffled coat. Most of the time his nose runs. Symptoms can include coughing, diarrhea, and signs of paralysis.

Treatment: Keep the hamster in a draft-free place at 69°–75°F, that is, where he really should always be housed, and get instructions from the veterinarian, who will probably prescribe antibiotics, vitamin drops, and cardiovascular stimulants. Follow the prescribed dosages very carefully and thoroughly.

## Meningitis (LCM: Lymphocytic Chorio-Meningitis)

This meningitis is a young-animal disease of golden hamsters, with low mortality. Uniform symptoms are rare.

Some characteristics are: The animal loses weight, he is drowsy, his coat ruffles, his movements are slow, and sometimes he develops conjunctivitis, which causes an aversion to light. He grows somewhat more slowly than a healthy animal. The condition seems to last for only about 3 weeks.

This is really a mouse disease, transmitted to hamsters in poorly controlled breeding stations. This disease can be transmitted to people, but most of the time it develops like a flu. More severe developments are rare but may occur.

Pregnant women must take care to avoid exposure; if transmitted, the disease can result in premature birth and malformation of the child. On the other hand, a hamster that has been in the home for a while and is more than 5 months old may generally be considered safe. Golden hamsters, upon recovery from the disease, do not become chronic carriers of the virus but are completely healthy.

# When Your Hamster Is Sick

If you want to be entirely safe, ask your pet store dealer to provide you with a young animal from a known LCM-free stock. It is to be hoped that under pressure of both buyers and dealers all breeders will ultimately control their stock. Of course LCM-free animals must be sheltered in an absolutely mouse-free environment to avoid new infections!

*Inheritable Diseases*

Animals with inheritable diseases are not used for breeding and are rarely offered for sale in pet shops, unless the inherited disease is not symptomatic.

*Parasites*

These do not thrive on well-fed and properly cared for hamsters.

*Broken Teeth*

These seldom occur if the hamster receives proper care and treatment. In any case, the teeth grow back. The teeth can grow too long when the animal does not have access to hard foods for constant gnawing (p. 32).

*Overgrown Claws*

A hamster's claws grow too long when the cage is too small and opportunities for digging and climbing are lacking (p. 14).

*Bite Wounds*

These are by no means always harmless. Serious altercations should be avoided by providing the most natural and stress-free living conditions possible. Separate animals at once if they appear to be hostile to each other.

*Blindness*

This condition occurs in older hamsters. With good maintenance they nevertheless stay cheerful and healthy.

*Death from Old Age*

Old animals that suddenly eat less, sleep a lot, and give the impression of feebleness should be allowed to die in peace without assistance from the veterinarian. This is especially true if the animal feels no pain, as is generally the case.

If necessary, separate the feeble animal from the partner (which may suddenly become aggressive). Give him his favorite foods regularly, especially yogurt and other "moist" foods, but don't force him to eat them.

# Reproduction and Breeding

## Essential Prerequisites: Large- or Small-Scale Breeding?

Perhaps you are entertaining the thought of developing a hamster stock and thus earning money. Do not imagine that this is an easy task!

Of course, it is only mass breeding that can be profitable in the long run. Large-scale breeding, however, is not an undertaking that can be carried on casually in just any location. Apart from quiet, properly temperature- and ventilation-controlled, and well-aired rooms (for temperature and humidity see p. 13), with draft-free and roomy cages, you need starting capital, patience, basic know-how, intuition in dealing with animals, reliable customers, and time!

Long vacations or even weekend trips become problematic, since it's hard to find someone who will knowledgeably and conscientiously tend for the hamsters in your absence. Epizootic diseases and mass deaths can be the consequence of faulty care!

If you want only to maintain a pair of hamsters and do not regard the expected offspring as a source of income, everything becomes simpler. But the vacation problem remains (pregnant and nursing animals tolerate no disturbance, no change of environment, no change of guardian). Also, *what becomes of the babies?* They should not go to a home where they will receive worse care than with you. They are little creatures and not merchandise, which one shelters where there is space. For these reasons I advise you to educate yourself *beforehand!* Without question it is easiest to

maintain a single hamster that, when you spend plenty of time with him, feels completely comfortable, even without a mate. It is also simple to maintain two sisters from the same litter. If they really can't tolerate each other, only a second cage is necessary to help work things out.

Finally, the decisive question of large- or small-scale breeding remains. I consider it feasible to raise hamsters or to breed a distinct race only if you have a solution for all the above-mentioned problems. Then this chapter will provide you with basic knowledge for the small-scale breeding of hamsters. Even for those who wish to keep a single animal, the descriptions of hamster family life will be of great interest.

Before undertaking large-scale breeding, it is most important that you first accumulate experience over a considerable period of time with just *one* pair, and, by reading the appropriate literature (see p. 69), broaden the knowledge that you have already gained from practical experience.

## Breeding Just One Pair

From the preceding discussion it is evident that for the average owner mass breeding of hamsters is unlikely to be feasible. Let us, therefore, consider the keeping of just a single pair.

Mixed-sex animals of the same hamster brood are tolerant of each other and can stay together in one cage of appropriate size (p. 39). Males and females from different broods require separate cages and are brought together only for mating. Only

38

# Reproduction and Breeding

properly nourished animals are capable of reproducing and breeding healthy youngsters. If there are difficulties, it pays to try giving wheat germ as a dietary supplement.

A female golden hamster should be 8–9 weeks old at the beginning of breeding; the male, somewhat older. With dwarf hamsters the ideal age for starting to breed is later, from 3 to 4 months. When siblings grow up together, they regulate this by themselves for the most part, and under these circumstances sexual activity begins relatively late.

Females that have babies too early do not have enough milk, do not bring them up properly, and in many cases are inclined to cannibalism (eating their babies).

*Albino-golden hamsters, Russian hamsters, and beige-colored golden hamsters* are normally so peaceful that males and females can be constantly cared for together even when babies are born and suckled right up to the independence of the young. These animals also become tame toward people especially fast; therefore I recommend them to beginners.

Of course the cage for a couple should be roomy, should have an area of at least 20 × 15 inches with a height of 12 inches, and in addition to the usual furnishings (p. 14) should have two houses with a floor and a folding roof.

The same is true for *dwarf hamsters.* You had best buy just two independent, healthy young animals from one litter, let them grow up together, and never separate them.

Even young animals from different families can often be induced to adjust to each other if handled with patience and common sense. Every now and then they should be brought together until the female is ready to mate and remains peaceable. Then the two can be left together for good. Whenever possible, the female should be younger than the male; the female, for example, should be 8 weeks old and the male from 10 to 12 weeks old.

Breeders and, for the most part, pet-store dealers can differentiate males from females even when they are young animals. In order that you yourself may also be knowledgeable, carefully study Figure 3.

With *striped hairy-footed dwarf hamsters* it is frequently possible even for a full-grown female to become fully accustomed to an adult male, but never with any other female.

My striped dwarfs are in this way a mated pair. Most of the time they sleep cuddled closely together, clean each other, tumble clumsily with each other in the cage, and don't even fight over food—and that's saying something!

It took a lot of effort to get this far! Again and again I would put the several-months-old female in the cage of the year-old male—the opposite procedure jeopardizes the life of the male, as the females are far more aggressive! Again and again the poor male was attacked and bitten, so that I had to send the pugnacious little lady back to her own cage, without delay and with the use of gloves. Finally, one night she was gentler and resisted him only half-heartedly. In the evening she threw him on his back while he was lying quite still, sniffed and licked his abdomen and genitals, threw herself on her own back, and let herself be sniffed and cleaned—mating foreplay instead of hostilities.

I took a chance on leaving them together. The next morning they crawled out one after the other, drowsy and yawning, from the same house and begged me for some mealworms.

With *fawn-colored golden hamsters* and *dappled golden hamsters,* males and females must be housed separately and brought together only for mating.

With dappled hamsters the "buck" is brought into a separately roofed cage (the upper side must be open) in the morning. In the evening, after he has been able to mark off his territory liberally with his scent, the female is put in.

With the not quite so aggressive fawn-colored animals the female is placed right in the male's cage in the evening. The best time for this is between 8 and 11 o'clock at night. In any event you must, protected by gloves, remain close by and put the female back in her own cage if she bites the buck or after copulation has taken place.

Things almost never work out the first time; usually the goal is achieved only after numerous attempts. This is one more reason why it is preferable to try "family-style breeding," that is, the mating of a sibling pair. Albinos, Russian hamsters, beige-colored golden hamsters, and dwarf hamsters can be bred successfully in this way.

## Courting and Mating

When the female is placed in the cover cage, she marks her territory with a secretion and drops of urine. Her abdomen is pressed tightly against the floor to achieve this.

The odor of this secretion varies, depending on whether or not the female hamster is in heat and ready to mate. The male hamster understands this sign

Figure 14 *Hamster couple at mating foreplay: each one reciprocally licks the head, ears, belly, and genitals of the other.*

immediately. Most of the time he even reacts properly and approaches only when his lady is ready. He begins courting: he licks her head and ears, nudges her with his nose, strokes her cheeks with his handlike, pink paws. In turn both lie on their backs and allow the partner to sniff and lick their abdomens and genitals (Figure 14). Then the female runs away, is pursued by the male, stops, is nudged in the side, and continues running. Finally the male tries, persistently and not at all gently, to raise the little hindquarters of the female with his snout until she becomes completely rigid and lets him have his way. After mating the rigidity subsides, and the female, by

40

# Reproduction and Breeding

nudging with her nose and encircling, exhorts the male hamster to renewed activity; the mating repeats itself several times as a rule.

## Pregnancy: What to Watch for

If a female is expecting only a few offspring, her belly's circumference increases so little that an inexperienced person can hardly notice it.

Changes in behavior are much more evident to attentive observers: the female noticeably hoards and buries food, works and digs in the nest (most of the time in the sleeping quarters), carries nesting material in and out, and is quite obviously engaged in padding everything freshly and softly. Many times she will build the nest in the cage. You must, therefore, provide sufficient fresh nesting material for this purpose.

During pregnancy many females are more nervous and timid than otherwise. Take this into consideration, and be especially calm and friendly with the animal. Avoid noises or sudden movements, and don't let strangers near her.

A protein- and vitamin-rich diet is now more important than before. In older females the embryos in the uterus may lose hold and be reabsorbed by the body, especially if the animals have been improperly fed.

Estimate—better yet, calculate—when the babies are due (see the next section), and change the straw about 2 days before. Afterwards wait until the babies are 10 days old in order not to disturb the mother.

Shortly before birth the male withdraws from the common nest and builds himself, in another corner of the cage, a bed in which he sleeps until the little ones are a few days old, even though the couple gets on very well together.

## Birth and the Nursing Period

Finally, one day it happens (with *golden hamsters* after 16–18 days, with *Chinese striped hamsters* after 20–22 days, and with *striped hairy-footed dwarf hamsters* after 19–20 days gestation). The mother hamster is not seen at the customary time, and those with good hearing can hear the fine, high-pitched peeping of the babies in the nest. Newly born *golden hamsters,* about six to eight in number, initially weigh only $\frac{1}{10}$ ounce; newborn *dwarf hamsters,* five to six in number, only $\frac{1}{20}$ ounce. Both breeds are hairless and blind.

Frightened hamster mothers may eat their own young, especially if they are inexperienced. Therefore this is the time to

Figure 15 *A hamster mother suckling very young babies. When the pups reach about 10 days of age, the mother nurses while standing.*

be especially quiet and watchful and to avoid all unnecessary bustling around the nest! Until the babies are at least 1 week old, only *the regular guardian* should change the straw in the urinal area. Nesting material may be changed only after the weaning of the babies—at the earliest, only after 3 or 4 weeks.

All during the evening you should make quick checks of the nest in order to make sure that everything is all right. Dead animals must be removed at once! The mother should not be in with her offspring when you do this lest she be disturbed. Tempt her away from her supervision with a morsel of food so that she is in another corner of the cage. Do not touch the live babies!

If you have followed all these instructions and the hamster mother still eats her young, the cause can be an inadequate diet. She requires a diet high in protein, moisture, and vitamins. At this time give vitamin drops regularly according to instructions and also offer some powdered milk mixed into paste in an easily cleaned bowl. The remains must be removed the next morning without fail, and the bowl must be washed thoroughly.

## Raising the Young

When I saw tiny, still blind baby hamsters for the first time, I marveled at how skillfully and quickly they moved around. A pup that had just nursed fell flat on the straw as the mother left the nest in expectation of a morsel of food. The baby, sure of his goal, then wriggled back to his

Figure 16  *If a baby hamster crawls around outside the nest, the mother carries him back again in her mouth.*

siblings, which he apparently could smell and whose warmth he could detect.

For the most part the mother of course grabs when a hamster baby crawls out of the nest. She takes hold of him somewhere and carries him back in her mouth (Figure 16) or in her pouches. The little one holds completely still, just as we have seen with kittens and puppies.

With dwarf hamster pairs the father often takes part in gathering up the children. At the age of 10–12 days, however, the little hamsters are already so independent that they resist and can no longer be carried. They generally develop rapidly, becoming noticeably more enterprising and more curious. At 8 days they are nibbling at the food that the mother carries in. At about 12 days they open their eyes, and shortly thereafter, when they are about 2 weeks old, the mother or both parents let them crawl wherever they want to. They return by themselves for water and warmth. Of course it is obvious that you cannot yet let them run around in the room!

At this age the baby hamsters play a great deal, especially in the first hours after the onset of twilight, but also often during

# Reproduction and Breeding

the day. Konrad Lorenz describes this in his book *He Spoke with the Cattle, the Birds and the Fish* in his inimitable way: "In a large box next to my desk a sextet of three-week-old, downright exaggeratedly sweet golden hamster babies are waging the funniest prizefights. The scarcely mouse-high fellows, which are little clods of fat, roll over and over and do so with a loud squeak as if they would bite each other dangerously. They chase each other in wild hops across the whole box, whereby they constantly fall over because they are still so awkward and clumsy." They are now in the "flea stage" and so appealing

Figure 17 *The golden hamster children are now at an age when they nibble at food that their mother carries in.*

that one would like to keep them all. But this is impossible, and it is time to ask the future owners to prepare everything in advance for the new house guests.

Three-week-old animals can indeed still stay with the mother, but it is no longer vital that they do so. In fact, if, soon after bringing forth her young, the mother hamster becomes pregnant again, she nips away the offspring that have grown big, because the new ones that she is expecting require all her attention.

In the wild the siblings stay together for a while. During this time, when they have not yet become "lone wolves," they adapt most easily to people. Adult golden hamsters attack all members of their species; every young animal knows that instinctively. In encounters with adult golden hamsters the young animal assumes, therefore, a definite position of surrender, in order not to be bitten: he goes around peg-legged on his hindfeet and turns his small hindquarters to the adult with his little tail stretched sharply upward. Thereupon males leave the weaker animals in peace, while females are often inhibited from attacking by a cry of fear. This protective stance is not completely forgotten upon arriving at maturity and has been observed more than once with weaker animals vis-à-vis superior ones.

In general, hamsters are sexually mature in 4–5 weeks, long before they finish growing. You already know, however, that they must not be used for breeding at this time (p. 39).

Golden hamsters are fully grown at the age of 3 months, and dwarf hamsters at 2 months. But they continue to increase in weight until they are a year old.

Plate 5 *Young field hamsters.*

# Special Chapter:
# Understanding Hamsters

## How Pet Fanciers Discovered Hamsters

In 1893 zoologists heard of *Cricetus auratus* for the first time. The discoverer, Waterhouse, named the animal in Latin from "golden hamster." All the zoologists got to see was a single golden hamster fur, which Waterhouse had donated to the British Museum.

Living specimens of *golden hamsters* were found 37 years later: in 1930 Professor Aharoni of the Zoological Department of the University of Jerusalem made an excursion into the Syrian Desert and—probably alerted by tracks—dug a golden hamster mother with eight babies out of their burrow. Four babies later escaped, and a female was killed by her brother. However, the surviving animals reproduced themselves, and by the end of the year there were 364 golden hamsters under human care.

At this time these hamsters received the scientific name which they currently bear, *Mesocricetus auratus,* gold-colored "middle" hamsters, because the animals are smaller than field hamsters *(Cricetus)* and bigger than dwarf hamsters *(Cricetulus).* Now scientists speak of Syrian golden hamsters.

Since the animals adjusted relatively quickly to cage life, were easy to care for and tame, and were extremely fertile, they soon began to be used as experimental animals. In the interest of breeding and maintaining experimental animals, many observations about suitable shelter, feeding, and treatment of golden hamsters were published in scientific magazines and handbooks. Later they became popular house pets, first in America and after 1945 in Europe.

The Chinese striped hamster, *Cricetulus griseus,* has been an experimental animal for bacteriological studies since 1919. In more recent times it has even been used for research in diabetes. Until 1936, Chinese and Mongolian researchers had to catch their experimental animals, sometimes in the yurts (round fur tents) of the nomads, or dig them out of their burrows. It was not until 1937 that an attempt was made to breed striped hamsters in the laboratory. This was not a success on the first try, but after a while scientists learned how the animals had to be quartered and what they needed in order to raise healthy babies. Since 1951 there has been a great interest in the United States in the breeding of this hamster species, and a few years later Chinese striped hamsters began to appear in European laboratories. Since 1971 they have been increasingly available in pet shops.

The striped hairy-footed dwarf hamsters, *Phodopus sungorus,* originate in the steppe regions of Siberia, North Kazakhstan, northern China, and Mongolia. They were mentioned in scientific publications as early as the 1920s. Striped hairy-footed hamsters also live in the vicinity of human settlements; they can even be caught in the nomads' tents. They were introduced to us in the 1960s, when their life rhythms, living habits, and reactions in the laboratory were studied. More recently these small, gentle hamsters can also be found in pet stores. However (just as in the case of the Chinese dwarf hamsters), breeding them is not as simple as breeding the golden hamster. The animals have fewer and smaller litters even under ideal conditions. If mistakes are made, there are generally no offspring, or the parents will not take care of them. This

Plate 6   *A field hamster on the alert.*

also explains the higher prices for these hamsters.

## Adjustment to the Desert Climate

Hamsters belong to the few animal species that can survive because of their ability to adjust to dry regions. *Golden hamsters* originate on the desert steppes with sparse yearly precipitation and unheard of differences in temperature between day and night; *dwarf hamsters* come from the tundra steppes, in which plant growth is possible only a few months of the year. *Chinese dwarf hamsters* have been caught above the tree line on top of a 515-foot-high mountain!

These species have survived only because they are frugal with the use of water in all of their vital functions. The mother's milk seems to be very concentrated, the urine contains little water, and the droppings are dry. Breeding and raising the babies are directly related to the time of the best availability of food. Even the number of babies is dependent on the food supply and the prevailing weather. Dwarf hamster males have smaller testicles and no spermatozoa (sperm cells) in winter—a sensible adaptation to the climate. If the hamsters remain still, they are hard to detect because their fur color is well adapted to the background—a protection against predators. In the winter the Siberian striped hairy-footed hamsters have white or whitish fur, so that they too are barely visible in the snow.

*Golden hamsters* live in the steppe regions and in the richly cultivated grain fields of Syria, where it is very hot all day long. They spend the day sleeping in a relatively cool underground burrow—the nesting chamber is about ¾ foot deep—and go out only at night in search of food. In this way they save water, which would otherwise be necessary for keeping cool.

At temperatures of 59°F the golden hamsters become sluggish; at 50°F they enter into a cold sleep. Of course exceptions prove the rule. The obviously very hungry young fugitive that turned up one beautiful, snowy, frosty winter's day on a food search (p. 26) luckily had not fallen asleep.

*Dwarf hamsters* are outside mainly at night during the short summers in their native countries. During the cold months, however, they travel more during the day. Winter temperatures are extremely low at night, and the deep, well-padded burrow provides a cozy shelter.

Dwarf hamsters do not hibernate, but they are less active at very low temperatures, as this saves energy. They weigh the most during July and August and the least during December and January.

## What Wild Hamsters Eat

Every wild hamster nourishes himself with dry seeds and small invertebrate animals: insects, insect larvae, and spiders, which are a source of important protein as well as special tasty morsels.

*Golden hamsters* only occasionally find an abundance of green food, namely, when it rains heavily. The plants that are adapted to this climate then grow explosively from seed, bloom, bear fruit, and then quickly vanish again.

In the short summer months *dwarf hamsters* have both one-year-old and older

47

grasses available. They also have various robust plants at their disposal. The composition of their food depends on the kind of local plant growth. The most important food plant is always the one that bears an abundance of seeds. Even very small seeds are taken if the supply is great enough.

Figure 18 *Young animals jousting; they jostle each other and try to knock each other over.*

At night all hamsters run long distances in order to find sufficient food, unless they live right in a grain field. However, even under the most favorable circumstances they cannot eat enough so that they will not be hungry until the next night. They frequently need supplemental feedings. Thus it is good that they can carry home in their roomy cheek pouches (which reach to their shoulders), seeds, insects, and crushed herbs and store them there in special storage rooms, for snacks and for times when not much that is edible is available.

Females must, of course, feed especially well. While they're having young and suckling them, there is less time for them to forage for food than normally. Perhaps this is why they are more aggressive toward their own species than are males.

Dwarf hamsters amass great amounts of provisions in the fall which they then must make do with for 7–9 months! The ripe seed is carefully sorted, and all matter such as husks that can spoil easily is removed. Dwarf hamsters also store protein food in the form of small animal life. In one hamster winter food storage bin the following were found alive in the dead of winter: 40 different beetles, 4 maggots, and 15 spiders.

## Social Behavior

All behavior patterns that contribute to an understanding between animals of the same species—friendly and hostile—are designated in behavioral research as social behavior. Very little is known about golden hamsters living in the wild. Thus we are mainly directed to observations in an artificially created, and therefore only seminatural, environment. Apparently the wild female tolerates the male only for mating and raises the babies alone. She fusses solicitously and lovingly with them until, after 3 or 4 weeks, they become self-sufficient. They are then chased away by biting. Only breeding and domestication have made it possible for pairs to live together peacefully on a permanent basis—and this is true only of the Russian-albino and beige-colored golden hamsters, not of all breeds!

For observation of the social behavior of male golden hamsters under approximately natural conditions, two animals were kept in an 80-square-foot enclosure in which they could also dig and build. During the first week each animal was left alone in one half of the space in order to have the opportunity to get used to everything and (by means of the secretion of a special

# Special Chapter: Understanding Hamsters

gland) to demarcate his territory. After the separating doors were opened, there was a wild battle. The weaker hamster finally fled back to his own half of the enclosure, and from that moment on he led a hard life. He scarcely dared to leave the immediate vicinity of his burrow, he could gather only limited food supplies, and only rarely did he mark off territory—and then only by his own nest.

The superior (dominant) male moved everywhere with freedom, stored up a great supply of food, and frequently marked off territory right up to the burrow of the weaker animal. Af first the loser of the battle would always defend his own nest, but after a while he generally would flee if the stronger of the pair forced his way in. In a caged relationship the weaker hamster would, without question, soon have been dead!

Chinese striped hamster females had the reputation for a long time of being "man-killing" Amazons. More recently, experienced breeders and keepers discovered that sibling couples from the same litter which were never separated would tolerate each other as adults and raise their young together. You cannot make previously unacquainted adult Chinese hamsters get used to each other, however, and you should not even attempt it. As these hamsters get older, they become more and more intolerant and snappish.

There have been interesting observations about the social behavior of Chinese striped hamsters. A few 5-month-old siblings that had never been separated were kept in an 80-square-feet enclosure where there were opportunities for digging and burrowing, just as in the experiment with golden hamsters. This resulted neither in serious quarrels nor in sexual contacts. Each hamster had his favorite spot, but they all made use of the whole area.

After the siblings were caged separately elsewhere, four animals that had grown up as strangers to each other, two females and two males, were placed in the enclosure. Each hamster had its own burrow and its own feeding place with pellets and water at its disposal. In addtion there was also a common feeding trough with especially popular, tasty food. At first the animals just sniffed at each other. This soon led to battles but without serious injuries. The vanquished could always save him- or herself by fleeing in the large enclosure. Then the hamsters explored the area, examined all the furnishings, carried in supplies, and cleaned each other thoroughly—which is often a sign of better relations to come. Soon afterward the males and females become interested in each other, leading to courtship play and mating, which the females insisted on. However, each animal continued to live alone and the couples never stayed together for very long.

After a while they all became domesticated in the enclosure, and grew accustomed to each other's presence. Thus they became calmer, and several times each night they ran around in the enclosure for about 10 minutes, each one at a different time. Forceful penetration into another's burrow resulted in violent battles, because the owner furiously defended his or her domain. Moreover, the weaker one, if not unexpectedly awakened from a deep sleep, could often drive out the stronger one in these cases. At the common dinner bowl, however, there was a positively fixed order of rank.

# Hamsters

It has also been established that females are almost always stronger and more aggressive than males and that battles between them are rare but more violent. With all hamsters, females have a different manner of fighting from males. Males leap at their opponents with lightning speed from any position; females run around first and then bite from the side.

Striped hairy-footed dwarf hamsters seldom bite, even in the wild, and they are by nature gentler and less bellicose among themselves than the other hamster species. Frequently even adult partners become habituated to each other (see p. 39).

A pair bond is formed only when both animals find each other congenial. For hamsters, which above all have an "odor picture" of their opposite number, congeniality means that they smell good to each other. Antipathy is never neutralized by the highly vaunted power of attraction of the sexes.

## Predatory Enemies

Apparently nothing is precisely known about the predatory enemies of the Syrian golden hamster. They are certainly numerous; otherwise one would literally have to stumble over golden hamsters at night, judging by the proverbial fecundity of the animals.

Dwarf hamsters have been observed in their natural milieu, and we know more about these animals. Birds of prey such as owls catch and consume these little hamsters, especially during the winter. If the dwarf hamsters move around, their color is no longer a protection—the animals cannot run under the surface of the snow like mice; they can only run on the snow, where they are clearly visible. They move about in search of food or from one food bin to another. These are often from 110–185 feet apart, and with their full cheek pouches the animals are really clumsy and thus easy to catch.

Predators and frequently a not too abundant supply of food have an effect on the supply of dwarf hamsters that causes their number to remain about the same over a long period of time.

Figure 19  *If a hamster feels inferior to his opponent, he will turn over and remain motionless on his back.*

## Grooming Behavior

"Grooming behavior" includes all types of animal behavior that pertain to the care and maintenance of physical well-being.

Hamsters place great stock on *cleanliness,* a trait that they have in common with other rodents. In the wild, they dig, besides passageways, living holes, nesting holes, and holes for food stores, also a special toilet area. Even in their cage they use only

# Special Chapter: Understanding Hamsters

a certain corner to dispose of urine. If their cage is not kept clean by the owner, and if the straw is not changed often enough, they frequently react with irritability and snappishness.

Hamsters cherish *comfort*. They pad their lair in the burrow warmly and softly, using dried, finely shredded plant fibers. A female that is expecting young throws out the old "bedding" and carries in new material, which is formed into a proper round nest.

Thus it is important that your animals always have sufficient nesting material at their disposal (p. 17). If it gets too warm for my striped hairy-footed dwarf hamsters during typical summer weather (although I keep them in the coolest room at that time), they drag their bedding out of the nesting box piece by piece and build themselves an airy nest in another place in the cage. This is "in the open," and they sleep there. "Camping out" is apparently more pleasant at high temperatures.

Fur care is essential to hamsters! One of the hamster's good habits is that, after awakening in the evening, he will wash himself thoroughly from head to foot and will repeat this process several times (perhaps somewhat more superficially) during the waking period. The hamster sits upright during this procedure, but not like a squirrel on his hindlegs, rather more on his little hindquarters. At first the constantly licked paws are used to wash the face. Then the paws and tongue clean and rub the stomach, back, front legs, and thighs—often with almost acrobatic twists. Head, ears, and the remaining fur are scratched bit by bit—the left side with the left rear foot, the right side with the right foot. Claws and toes are carefully licked.

Hamsters have their own "table manners": they hold their food very deftly with their handlike paws, and they also use them to take food that is offered, such as mealworms, crickets, and peanuts. Small bites are taken from lettuce leaves held in the paws and eaten.

## Sound Language

If you have good ears, you can hear hamster babies squeaking in the nest: in quarrels over food and their places at the mother's warm, soft belly. The mother, which, contrary to us, can hear even in the supersonic range, always reacts to these sounds and fetches back individual children as quickly as possible when they have gotten out of the nest and are calling for help.

Adult hamsters under no stress are for the most part mute, at any rate to our ears. Of course I think it is possible that they "say" more than we can hear—certainly in the ultrasonic range and thus inaudible to us. Unfortunately I don't know whether there is any research on this topic.

The following sounds are well known and easily audible to us:

- The grunt-squeak, a mixture of grunting and squeaking, uttered in anger immediately before and during serious altercations.
- Teeth chattering, an expression of aggression and stern warning in the direction of the foe before and during attack.
- Shrieking, an expression of resistance and great fear in animals that are sorely pressed by an adversary or a predatory foe.

● Squeaking, an utterance of slight anger without serious meaning during quarrels between pairs that understand each other well.

## Body Language—Odor Language

Everyone who has ever been concerned with this subject knows that one can unknowingly express many things not only by words but also by mannerisms, bearing, and movement. With human beings, these "garnishings," along with the tone of the voice, enter into every conversation. The partner reacts, often unconsciously, in a positive or negative way, to the emotional "toppings."

Hamsters cannot speak, their sound language is, as far as we know, really simple, and they likewise have no mannerisms. Therefore body language plays an especially great role with them. It gives them the opportunity to express intelligibly, for their species (and also for us), what they feel. But please don't misunderstand this statement as humanizing this behavior into "conscious communication"!

● Convulsive movement, as well as sudden continual face washing, signifies fright.

● Defensive raising of both front paws can be observed in males that have been unexpectedly attacked by females and have no way of escaping. According to my observations, this gesture prevents or at least delays an even more serious attack.

● Puffing up the cheeks and showing the abdominal regions are to be construed as a threat.

● Lying motionless on the back shows resistance and fear (Figure 19).

● Stiff-legged walking of a young animal, with its tail stiffly stretched straight up and its hindquarters turned toward the adult hamster, denotes fear and submission (Figure 20); it propitiates the old animals. This can also often be observed in vanquished adult hamsters.

Figure 20 *Surrender position of young golden hamsters: they turn their raised hindquarters, with stiffly upraised tail, toward the adult hamster.*

● Stretching and yawning with half-closed eyes is an expression of cosiness and inner peace, just as much as frequent and at the same time joyous and langorous washing.

● Reciprocal cleaning between mother and children, and also between males and females, that live in harmony with each other indicates affection.

● Stroking the head with a paw, sometimes for a long period and sometimes only quickly and in passing, denotes tenderness. I observed this frequently with my striped hairy-footed hamster couple; the male constantly stroked the female, which seemed to enjoy this tender little act.

# Special Chapter: Understanding Hamsters

- Reciprocal knocking over can have very different meanings: fighting, if there is biting; coital foreplay, if the animals lick each other's stomachs and genitals; playing, if the partners cavort around with each other for a short time only.
- "Sitting up" is sometimes noticed, if something excites the hamster's particular attention.

A specific "scent picture" of the environment of the species, and of the male or female owner, is much clearer to rodents and more important than anything that they perceive visually. These animals have the opportunity, by means of secretion of odors, to express moods and·to impart "messages" to companions.

Male and female golden hamsters have scent glands on their sides. With these secretions, after much sniffing, they demarcate particularly areas where others have already fought.

According to everything that is known, *rubbing the sides* is not a direct threat nor does it serve to bring the sexes together. However, it does have a relationship to aggressiveness and a feeling of superiority: males that had been victorious in battle with other males or had fought with females not in heat (less violent) demarcated a great deal. Vanquished males, on the other hand, hardly demarcated at all. Even dominant males, however, demonstrate hardly any demarcation behavior after contact with females in heat. Interest in the females seems to affect this behavior—the males now have something else on their mind.

Females in heat mark off their territory with secretions from their genitals, which they press firmly to the ground. Males then get the message: I can approach this female without any great risk.

Females not in heat likewise dab scent marks on the ground when a male approaches, at first only very fleetingly. If they should nevertheless be pursued, they demarcate with great thoroughness and at very short intervals, until the male gives up or the female becomes aggressive with her paw.

Males and females of the Chinese striped hamster variety have side and stomach glands (ventral glands) whose secretions they use for demarcation of their territories.

Males and females of the striped hairy-footed dwarf species possess only abdominal glands, whose secretions are detectable even by human noses. With them they designate territories as their own, even though they may be unaware of this action. After a certain period of adjustment the demarcation stops. Only when people appear who are strange (and, to the hamsters, unpleasant smelling) do the hamsters again start to lay down scent.

Figure 21 *Even the field hamster, which is, of course, unsuited to being kept in the house, is "alerted" when something attracts his attention.*

# Hamsters

## Seeing, Hearing, Touching, Smelling

**Seeing** plays a subordinate role with hamsters, somewhat similar to the sense of smell in a human being. Also, they cannot distinguish colors.

**Hearing** is good (not just in the supersonic range), and every hamster quickly learns to distinguish the voice of his owner from that of other people. If he isn't in a deep sleep, he will come expectantly out of his nest as soon as he is called by a person familiar to him—often even if he isn't called but just hears the voice.

**The well-developed sense of touch**, along with the "tool" of sensing hairs, enables hamsters to determine promptly whether or not they can force their way through a space or a crevice.

Hamsters in captivity sometimes remain in a hidden location. This is especially true if they were frightened and ran away. Thus it will be better if, before the first excursion of your hamster in the house, you remove all possible pitfalls or, better still, choose a safe room in which he can run around.

The **faculty of smelling** is so enormously differentiated that we can hardly imagine its power. If two strange hamsters are put together in the same cage, a profuse sniffing of the scent traces is the first thing that happens—all other activities come later.

Hamsters experience their environment, members of their species, their predatory enemies, and above all the people around them as specific combinations of odors. They perceive their surroundings, their partner, or their adversary exclusively in terms of odor, and not, as we do, in terms of image. Good relationships between sisters from one litter or between a pair swiftly turn into furious enmity if one animal is separated for any length of time from the other, if it is brought into a strange-smelling environment, if it is carried around by people, or if it is placed together with another hamster. We must be aware of this and make sure that the group odor of animals that have tolerated each other (and who will be staying together) does not disappear.

The group odor does disappear when the hamsters in a cage are separated by wire netting and no longer have the chance to reciprocally clean each other and to sleep cuddled up to each other. Sisters can no longer be reconciled to each other, and couples become readjusted only with much patience and frequent attempts (and by making use of the female's heat).

Occasional *voluntary* sleeping apart, which I notice more often with my dwarf hamster couple, doesn't do any harm.

Even if you keep only *one* hamster, you probably have to take into consideration his sensitivity to smell. Many animals show a marked negative reaction if they are fed by hands that smell of other animals, especially other rodents. They react nervously and snappishly. Just one thing helps: wash your hands thoroughly before you feed your hamster!

## Sense of Orientation

Every hamster explores a new environment quickly and thoroughly by means of his senses of smell and touch. This is "ingrained in him" because it is vitally important for young animals that, for example, must look for a new home to know as soon as possible where there are hiding places, where they can dig a burrow, and where they will be able to find adequate food.

Even domesticated hamsters still possess this trait. If they are not disturbed and frightened, after a short while they move around in a new cage with great matter-of-factness. But they also become well acquainted with the household rooms which they regularly can run around in. There they soon acquire a preference for definite places: for the wastebasket, which they can climb up agilely in order to get to the couch and thereby reach the shoulder or lap of a person; for a very definite place on the wall, where the wallpaper is easily removed and can be chewed to pieces; for the space between wall and bookcase, in which it is possible for an inveterate climber to behold people from above; for the vicinity of the door, which from their experience always opens and reveals a greater domain. Both of the last two preferences present dangers—therefore be careful!

## Anatomical Characteristics

### Hamster Pouches

Hamster pouches are capacious bags of skin that reach to the shoulders. When they are empty, they are not at all noticeable; but with completely full cheek pouches a hamster looks downright deformed. Provisions are carried in the hamster pouches, and even small babies in time of danger (Figure 22).

### Incisor Teeth and Chewing Muscles

Like all rodents, hamsters have rootless incisors that grow throughout their lifetime. One could really envy them for this! The teeth are shaped similarly to sharp-cornered chisels. Hamsters don't make as great use of the front teeth, which are covered on the side with enamel.

The chewing musculature is especially

Figure 22  *Provisions (and even offspring in times of danger) are carried in the hamster pouches, bags of skin that reach to the shoulders.*

Figure 23  *Hamsters skillfully use their muscular forepaws with the four "fingers" and a rudimentary thumb for digging, climbing, hanging, and polite eating.*

strongly developed and is set into the powerful jawbones.

### Legs, Fingers, Toes

The forelegs of the golden hamster, with four "fingers" and a rudimentary thumb, are powerful and muscular. The hamster digs with them, and uses them for climbing and hanging on the wire of his cage (Figure 24). The weaker hindlegs, with five well-developed toes, push the excavated earth to the rear and serve as supports in climbing.

Figure 24 *A very popular hamster game: hanging upside–down from the wire-mesh roof of the cage.*

*Big Eyes*

The black gleaming eyes, which are especially large in dwarf hamsters, protrude a little, as with most nocturnally active animals.

## Ability to Learn

Hamsters get to know people who have a lot to do with them. This is not true in the complicated sense that people know each other—they take note of odor and voice. Their reactions to different people reflect good and bad experiences that are closely associated with them in the hamster's mind.

Hamsters can orient themselves well in rooms and learn to find their way around in a new environment quickly. But they also take note of places, for example, a place where they once or twice enjoyed a specific morsel of food. Later they beg precisely on that spot if they get hungry again. For example, my striped hairy-footed hamster male climbs onto his sleeping house when he wants mealworms, whereas his female climbs 16 inches high on the front mesh in order to eat her "worm" in my cupped hand, after I have carefully taken her off the mesh. Underneath this acrobatic-wire spot, I place, of course, an especially thick layer of wood shavings because, despite all her dexterity, she still tumbles down from time to time.

Practically all hamsters will voluntarily use their running wheels and other exercise gear (p. 17). This is also a learning procedure—indeed, an especially important one.

The animals are also extremely resourceful and persistent when it comes to getting exotic-looking food crumbs into the nest. Thus Harry, a hamster that belonged to friends, found a large walnut on the floor during his evening excursion. He could scarcely grip it with his teeth. He didn't give up, however, and with great and downright acrobatic efforts he transported it into his cage and from there into his sleeping house.

I don't think it is desirable to teach hamsters clever tricks thought up by people. It degrades the animals to clowns or playthings and deprives us of the pleasure of learning something of their real nature.

# Gerbils (Mongolian Desert Mice)

## The Origin and Characteristics of Gerbils

In England and the United States, "gerbils," as they are called in these countries, have been popular house pets since the 1960s (current price here about $6). Lately they have become available in continental Europe also.

It is quite possible that you have seen those Mongolian desert mice in a pet shop. People who look at them hastily generally consider them to be mice; more careful observers regard them rather as a new type of squirrel. Zoologically, however, they belong to the burrowing animals. They are therefore related closely to the hamster and only remotely to mice and squirrels.

There are many strains of gerbils in the dry regions of North Africa, Israel, Palestine, Arabia, Iran, Turkey, and Russia. Of course they are of various sizes and exhibit various types of social behavior; externally, however, they are very simliar to one another.

The gerbil, or Mongolian desert mouse, the easternmost representative of this species in general, lives in the steppe regions of Mongolia and northern China, and on Lake Baikal. The head-to-rump length measures 4–4¾ inches, and the muscular tail is 2½–4¾ inches long. The body is slender, yet at the same time stocky; the head is relatively short and broad. The gleaming black eyes protrude slightly, the ear flaps are somewhat enlarged, and the decorative whiskers and the little nose are in constantly sniffing motion.

While eating, gerbils sit on their very powerful, elongated hindlegs so that they can carefully observe their surroundings. The front paws, with "black lacquered" claws in the adult animals, are used very skillfully as hands in eating and in carrying nesting material. The tail is completely piliated and ends in a kind of brush or the suggestion of a tuft. The smooth, silkily gleaming fur in healthy animals is golden brown toward the surface, and is interspersed with evenly distributed, darker hairs. Breast and abdomen have thick, whitish fur.

Gerbils differ markedly from other types of mice in that they have a small naked spot near the heel at the otherwise fully furred soles of the hindfeet.

They have only dry droppings and produce little urine, excreting both almost soundlessly. Since, in contrast to other mice, they have been bred often and therefore are frequently available, I will concern myself here only with this species.

Despite their closeness to hamsters, including some common qualities, there is a series of differences in nature and the necessities of life that you should know about if you wish to keep a gerbil.

## One Gerbil or a Pair?

This question brings us to the first difference. Gerbils, unlike hamsters, are not "lone wolves." The owner of a single animal, therefore, must be prepared to spend time with his or her animal and not be too heavily preoccupied with other matters. You should devote time daily to the animal as long as it lives (6–8 years); otherwise it will become apathetic or snappish. It doesn't tolerate being left alone. Therefore you had best plan to buy two sisters from the same litter. Hopefully the breeder or dealer knows the not too simple art of determining the sexes of young animals! Experience has shown that gerbil sisters tolerate each other all their lives; they play with one another, clean each other reciprocally, and sleep snuggled closely together. With animals from different families and from different origins, however, you will unfortunately always run a risk. Choosing an unrelated pair can often lead to a deadly altercation.

Maintaining two females also saves you the headache of housing the numerous progeny that is to be expected regularly from a male and a female.

Brothers are also basically peaceable with each other, but it's not entirely certain whether living together constantly without harm is possible, even if they are housed in a large cage. I know of two brothers that after a while ate each other's tails, and I would therefore counsel against trying to keep males together.

Couples tolerate each other all their lives, stay very close together, grieve when they are separated, and still recognize each other after having lived apart for several weeks (up to 3 months). The babies are cared for by both.

Females whose males have died are for the most part not ready to live together with another male.

Recognition after a long time and the refusal of a new partner also apply to a pair of sisters. If one of the animals dies, the owner must show great concern for the survivor. He must not only feed her but also stroke her and give her companionship and frequent excursions outside the cage. Otherwise she will languish, and grow fat and apathetic.

## Gerbils Need Lots of Room

Gerbils are as agile as weasels. They are also temperamental and curious. In pet shops they act sluggish and a little bored—but don't be fooled. Normally the animals spend just a short time there; they are not yet adjusted and have little room at their disposal, as that is generally the way things are set up.

Gerbils in the wild construct artistic and extensive passageways and crevices and place great value on living comforts, such as a soft and warmly padded nest. Even as domestic animals they need abundant opportunity for burrowing, burying, gnawing, working. Work for them is just as much a necessity of life as play. They require plenty of room for running and jumping. They like to dash around, and they are able to leap 16 inches in width and 12 inches high without effort.

## An Aquarium for a Home

A frame aquarium (Figure 25), *at least* 13–14 inches high and with an area of 24 × 12 inches, is a suitable gerbil home for two animals. Of course the gerbils feel that the bigger the aquarium is, the better. Both my

# Gerbils (Mongolian Desert Mice)

animals live in a cage 32 × 14 × 16 inches, and I don't have the feeling that it is too big.

Be sure that the putty of the aquarium is soft, like rubber, not hard. Hard putty has a lethal effect, even if only minute bits are gnawed off and inadvertently swallowed. Therefore you must take this into consideration even more with gerbils than with hamsters.

Perhaps you'll find someone who has a suitable but no longer completely watertight aquarium standing around in the cellar and will part with it cheaply. Otherwise you must spend a little more; or if you are a skilled amateur builder, you can construct the aquarium yourself. Even less handy individuals can prepare the indispensable airy roof out of galvanized wire mesh. Cages should have a very high floor surface (at least 5 inches), be made of the materials mentioned for hamsters (p. 14), and have the stated minimum area. Such cages will probably not be ideal, as the opportunities for building for gerbils have been very limited.

The cage for the gerbils, which are active day and night, should be illuminated. It's good to bring the cage (securely closed!) out on the terrace or the balcony from time to time. Do this during dry, sunny weather. The animals tolerate this well and like to take sunbaths, delightedly lying flat on their stomachs or even on their backs, but they must always have the opportunity to retreat into the shade. Continually check on them, because periods of sun and shade alternate. Overheating has killed many domestic animals whose owners were not sufficiently attentive. Dry air (40% relative humidity) at room temperature (66–70°F) is well tolerated.

*Equipment*

Gerbils need a relatively large sleeping house made of wood with a floor and a foldable roof. This is not difficult to make.

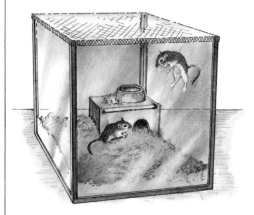

Figure 25 *The proper home for gerbils: a frame aquarium with a roof made of wire mesh. It should have an area of 24 × 12 inches and a height of at least 12 inches. Gerbils can effortlessly leap 16 inches in length and 12 inches high.*

The area should be 5 × 4 inches, the height should be 6 inches, and the side slip-through entrance should have a diameter of 2½ inches.

A running wheel is not absolutely necessary and is not even used by many animals. On the other hand, large pieces of decorative cork for passageways and burrows are much more important for gerbils than for hamsters. You can also supplement the equipment with small

59

branches, twigs, and roots, which can be found in fields. Of course, the roots must be cleaned with hot water before giving them to the gerbils. Everything will be fully gnawed through eventually and must then be replaced.

Be sure to provide your gerbils with a layer of wood chips at least 4–5 inches deep. It is sufficient to change it every 4 weeks. The best nesting material is good hay. The gerbils shred it finely, pack it more or less thickly (based on room temperature), and carry it to be "aired" in front of their sleeping house. Dry sand (clean sand from a construction company) in a dish without sharp edges, big enough so that a gerbil can fit in it comfortably, will be gladly used for sand baths by these animals accustomed to living in the wild. Sharp-pointed sand (such as that used for birds) damages the fur.

## Basic Rules for Maintenance and Care

As regards maintenance and care, gerbils in general are no different from hamsters (p. 20), but I would like to call your attention to a few peculiarities.

Gerbils are friendly and curious, but they like to chew on fingers—although most of the time without injuring the skin. Don't take this to heart; it is not meant in anger. Animals that have bad experiences or that suffer from a protein deficiency can become snappish, but this rarely happens. In the first instance, a great deal of patience is needed; in the second instance, a properly compounded diet often helps after a while.

Gerbils, in contrast to hamsters, are active both day and night. This means that very active play and work times alternate around the clock with rest and sleep times.

When the animals have gone to sleep, be sure to leave them completely in peace—you can occupy yourself with them when they are awake. Feed them, stroke them gently with one finger over their heads and backs, and rub their ears lightly. Let them sniff your fingers and climb on your hand. Raise your hand with the animal up just a bit, and then lower it gently so that he can climb off.

Provision for vacation periods may be made as in the case of hamsters.

*Playing and Exercise*
You can permit your gerbils to run

Figure 26 *You can grasp your gerbil firmly; push him carefully into a cage corner and place your hands over him like a roof.*

Figure 27 *Enfold the animal with a gentle squeeze, and lift him up with both hands.*

# Gerbils (Mongolian Desert Mice)

around the room by the hour (under supervision) only after they have become hand tame and understand the function of your hand as an "elevator." If you have a pair, both animals may, of course, run together. Place the sleeping house so it is accessible! Gerbils gnaw and bite on paper, wood, and textiles—much more than hamsters, so a room without furniture and wallpaper is ideal for the excursion.

At first, of course, they don't give much thought to their new surroundings. Even later on, they run and jump a great deal, as their motor urge is great! If an animal is placed all by himself in a strange room and without his familiar little house within reach, at first he frequently becomes paralyzed with fear. This can lead to an acute circulatory weakness. In such cases put the animal back in the cage immediately. Do this carefully, without frantic haste!

Many people seem to regard the gerbil's long, powerful tail as a useful handle. The animals should never be lifted up in this way, not even near the base of the tail. This hurts them, of course, and it can easily lead to fractures, which heal poorly and crookedly. Gerbils are as agile as weasels; you must therefore be especially careful not to step on them or to squeeze them.

All the information that you find in the sections entitled "Fun or Business?," "Hamsters and Other Domestic Animals," and "How You Can Avoid Accidents" (pp. 22, 25, and 26) holds true also for gerbils.

Gerbils need empty cardboard rolls from toilet paper, twigs, and branches much more than do hamsters, but they also like to chew blocks of wood (unpainted), whole walnuts, and pieces of wood.

*Proper Food*

Gerbils receive almost the same food as hamsters. It consists of mixed seeds, coarse rolled oats, vegetables, fruit, other greens, and nuts. Twigs and hay for nibbling and gnawing are even more important for gerbils than for hamsters and should be at their disposal as often as possible. Bark is peeled off expertly and neatly from wood while the gerbil is sitting on his haunches, carried to the mouth with the paws, and then eaten with pleasure. In the winter, you can cut suitable twigs and branches, strewing them in the cage as well as letting the gerbil feed on them. Hay is equally important for nourishment and nesting material. Mealworms are eaten only by adult animals, of about 3 months. The expensive grasshoppers and the cheaper crickets are available in many pet stores as food for large reptiles. Multivitamin drops should be measured out according to body weight, just as with hamsters, and it is best to dispense them on a mealworm.

For the most part water is not taken. However, there must always be sufficient fruit and vegetables such as apples, orange slices, carrots, and thick slices of cucumber at the animals' disposal. These should be rotated. Be sure to remove what is left over the next day! Even gerbils are thirstier than usual on torrid days and during hot spells, and this must be taken into account.

*Potential Signs of Nutritional Imbalance*

The incidence of disease has been, up to now, low in gerbils, probably because they

Plate 7 *A golden hamster couple in a mock fight.*

are still barely domesticated. What must be feared is diarrhea from wet or decayed food and symptoms of nutritional deficiency from a poorly balanced diet without the addition of vitamins, as well as fatty degeneration in overfed animals. Animals that have too little opportunity for plenty of movement and activity are in particular danger of the last-named ailment. Deficiency symptoms include shaggy fur, falling fur, uneven, delayed replacement of fur, crippling of the hindlegs, and the death of young animals.

## Breeding and Rearing

Friends of mine had the experience that one of their two gerbil sisters surprised them with offspring soon after purchase. The "aunt" was visibly helpful in the care of the little ones. She carried escapees back into the nest, warmed and cleaned them, and played with them.

Of course, this was charming to behold. But after a while there was the question that always arises in the maintenance of couples: What to do with the progeny? For this reason, as a matter of principle, I recommend keeping two sisters, which for the most part have no babies. Otherwise there are the same problems as with hamsters (p. 38). These are problems that should be resolved *before* the start of breeding. Young animals that have become independent should be given a comfortable existence for as long as they live, and not be handed over to people who very soon will barely concern themselves about them. When gerbils live in colonies, it is theoretically possible to maintain family groups of eight to ten animals.

Unfortunately, the family does not stay at this number, and the population problem looms up in a short time. (This will give you an idea of the reproduction rate: A young friend received a pair of gerbils for a Christmas present. Six months later he owned 28 animals, and with much handwringing he was looking for good homes for them!)

In addition you would need a cage with an area of about 60 square feet for such a group or a correspondingly big gnawproof and burrowproof room equipped with everything that gerbils need for living and activity. Neither of these is practicable for the average individual. Indeed, it is not at all simple to shelter even two gerbils in a style commensurate with their needs!

Of course, if you have prospective customers who understand and love animals, you may buy a pair. Your best choice would be two young animals that are accustomed to each other either as siblings or through common maintenance by the dealer. If they get to know each other only as adult animals, there are often difficulties. It is possible that they cannot stand the smell of each other and must be separated to prevent them from seriously injuring or even killing each other.

Congenial couples are very friendly with each other. The female often exhorts her partner to clean her by shoving her head under his snout while lying on her back. The male then very gently licks and nibbles the chin of his female, her tail, her abdomen, and her sides. Meanwhile the female closes her eyes and enjoys the caresses—until she has had enough. She then leaps up and protests against further

cleaning with a soft drumming of her forelegs. The whole episode generally ends with a short, friendly scuffle.

One more thing may be noticed among siblings. The relationship between the animals is apparently preserved and strengthened by stress situations. I have observed again and again with my gerbil sisters that each one would sniff the face of the other and press close to her for greater security in such situations.

*Mating*

Gerbils in the mating mood drum especially often with their hindlegs; this, to judge by the reaction of unconcerned animals, sounds different from the well-known warning drumming. This is true, at any rate, to the gerbils' ears. Before mating, the male chases after the female for a long time until, by bending down and lifting her hindquarters, she makes it possible for him to copulate with her. Only after repeated, constant, seconds-long copulation does the flow of semen occur, and after each instance the animals clean and lick each other's genitals intensively. During each period of heat in the female the act of copulation is repeated many times. Female gerbils can have babies up to the age of 14–20 months.

*Pregnancy and Nest Building*

Pregnant female gerbils generally increase in girth visibly and rapidly. Nonetheless they remain as agile, nimble, and graceful as before. The gestation period lasts about 24 days. A few days before the birth of the babies the female, with the help of the male, starts to build a new, especially well padded nest, normally in the sleeping box previously described. Good hay is also ideal at this time for nesting material.

*Birth, Nursing, Raising the Young*

The young gerbils, generally five to eight in number, come into the world naked, blind, and deaf and weighing about $\frac{1}{10}$ of an ounce. The ears are still close to the body, the limbs and the tail are short, but the feet and toes are already developed. The mother frees the newborn by nibbling on the embryonic sac, which she eats. She then licks the little one with her warm, powerful tongue over his entire body. Thus the breathing mechanism is properly activated, circulation is encouraged, and soon the baby makes his first nibbling movements toward the maternal nipples.

Even with hand-tame animals one must be sure not to disturb them during or shortly after birth, either by curious inspection or by noise of any kind. Otherwise the mother often becomes so frightened that she begins to eat the little ones. Many a litter has perished in this manner. During and shortly after the birth the father gerbil generally does not stay in the common nest, but rather remains in a makeshift home in another corner of the cage. However, this doesn't last long, and soon the whole family is living together again, with the father participating in the child rearing, especially by carrying back any escapees. Later he plays with the youngsters and "settles" quarrels.

Right after birth, however, the question is not one of escape. Only 2–5 days after birth the ear muscles strengthen. The tiny fur grows from the sixth day, while the whiskers (feelers) are visible by the twelfth day. The eyes open between the sixteenth and twentieth days. Even before they see, the little ones start to cavort around outside the nest. With the help of their senses of touch and smell, they can find their way back into the nest, but more often they are dragged back by the mother or father.

My "single-parent" female (the male died shortly before the birth) blocked the entrance to the nest when the confusion became too much for her and she had accommodated all the babies in the nest. Working from the outside, she pressed into place, with her forehead, the material that closed the entrance to the nest, and then retreated to a corner of the cage. There she cleaned herself lavishly, and, at peace, stretched out, yawned, and then slept to recover from the strain of child care. Soft but clear chirping soon woke her again—the little ones were hungry.

When living in the wild, covering up the nest and sealing it shut serves as a protection against predatory enemies. After each feeding, the young gerbils are thoroughly washed by the mother and, by means of her licking their abdomens and genitals, are induced to pass excrement and urine. This is quite customary with many nursing mothers; they lick everything up, and the nest stays clean.

As soon as the gerbil youngsters have their eyes open, they begin to chase each other with awkward leaps and to spring like fleas, with all four legs in the air at the same time. They sit up, somewhat unsteadily, and rap "alarm" when the parents rap—a not-to-be ignored chorus.

When I had to put my gerbil family in the bedroom for a while, their gnawing and scratching often disturbed me. If I said "Shhh," all the gerbils began to rap simultaneously—and this with some persistence! They soon had me so well trained that I remained quiet. In the flea stage young gerbils start carrying in and chewing on stalks of hay and also soon begin cracking open sunflower seeds. They test their digging and building ability communally on comical little "children's dens." They play and climb in these until suddenly the whole herd gets tired and forms a "sleeping pile," in which it is impossible to tell what belongs to whom. After 4 weeks the youngsters are so self-reliant that it is possible to separate them from the parents. With larger litters of over six young ones a couple of days more should be allowed.

It is best for the siblings to stay together until they have found a new home. In no case should they be placed singly— fortunately this is also known to pet-shop owners.

## Understanding Gerbils

Gerbils (Mongolian desert mice) are originally animals of the Mongolian and Chinese arid steppes. Today they are found also as civilization followers in relatively arid regions where crops such as buckwheat are cultivated.

Provisions are taken in only during the fall and are stored for the winter. The gerbils live in colonies, and neighbors are compatible with each other. Pair bonding is apparently the rule, and each pair has its

# Gerbils (Mongolian Desert Mice)

own spacious burrow in which the children live together with the parents until maturity. The fathers also concern themselves with the children right from the beginning. During the summerlike half year the adult females have babies about every 4 to 5 weeks. This frequency, however, does not result in overproduction, because the many predatory enemies (foxes, polecats, condors, and owls) make sure that only a few animals survive their first winter—probably the most alert, most careful, and most agile. Attentiveness and constant readiness for flight are, next to pronounced curiosity, essential characteristics of all desert mice. They like to observe the environment while sitting up on high points of land. At the least suspicious movement they drum loudly with their hindlegs and flee lightning-quick into the burrow. Even the members of the colony react to this warning signal, which can be heard far and wide on the steppe ground.

*Sound Language—Body Language—Odor Language*

Drumming with the hindlegs in a peculiar galloping rhythm, mainly with a definite drum-roll effect, is also observed in tame gerbils and is a signal of excitement. This production of sound reminds me of the drumming of rabbits which live both as pairs and in colonies. The gerbil drumming does sound a little different, but it has the same meaning.

The high-pitched chirping of young gerbils sounds like the twittering of baby birds, not like the squeaks of mice. It is clearly perceptible to the human ear.

Adult animals chirp in sexual agitation. My two mature gerbil sisters are often to be heard arguing.

Scientific research by means of supersonic equipment has revealed that these are not the only sounds. On the contrary, gerbils are extremely "chatty"; as typical social beings, they twitter, chirp, and peep almost continually as they meet or reciprocally clean each other.

Gerbils also have a body language. They can express various moods by means of posture and movements.

- Sitting upright on their powerful hindlegs, as if petrified, with their front paws close to each other and clenched into fists shows agitation, fright, and readiness to flee.
- The same posture without the stiffness and clenching signifies curiosity and anticipation.
- Leaping into the air with all fours at the same time is a sign of exuberance, as is playful boxing with the front paws.
- However, boxing with the front paws can also be serious and has occurred in genuine battles between animals that were strangers to each other. Such battles have resulted in injuries.
- A stiffly propped-up tail that is enthusiastically bent upward indicates venturesomeness.
- Thorough, leisurely cleaning of the face, abdomen, back, and tail, which is held tightly and elegantly with the paws, show inner tranquility.
- "Running under" the befriended partner, an action in which one animal, lying on its back with its throat pointed

upward, pokes under the snout of the other, is an exhortation to social, friendly cleaning.

- A short mutual licking sideways on the mouth is a kind of greeting.
- Reciprocal pushing away with the heads held close to each other is the beginning of a not-quite-friendly scuffle, which may arise, for example, when a male with the intention of mating approaches a nursing female that is not ready to mate.

Odor language is still another method of communication among the animals. Every gerbil has some kind of scent gland with which it demarcates its territory. The secretions are clear to gerbils, but are undetectable by human noses.

*Sensory Abilities*

The *faculty of smell* is also well differentiated and precise in desert mice, and the *sense of touch* is well developed. The animals can *hear* perfectly, including low-frequency sound.

According to my observations they *see* better and more precisely than hamsters. This may be connected with the fact that they are also wide-awake and active during the day.

Their *faculty of orientation* is excellent. In unfamiliar rooms gerbils soon find their way.

Gerbils are especially lovable animals. I hope that this chapter contributes to a better understanding of their individuality and their natural requirements in order that owners and animals will enjoy each other.

# Index

# Index

# Perfect for Pet Owners!

## "Clear, concise…written in simple, nontechnical language." —*Booklist*

ISBN prefix: 0-8120

## PET OWNER'S MANUALS

72-80 pages, paperback, 6½" x 7⅞" with
over 50 illustrations (20-plus color photos)

BANTAMS Fritzsche (3687-5)
CANARIES Frisch (2614-4)
CATS Fritzsche (2421-4)
COCKATIELS Wolter (2889-9)
DACHSHUNDS Fiedelmeier (2888-0)
DWARF RABBITS Wegler (3669-7)
FEEDING AND SHELTERING
  EUROPEAN BIRDS von Frisch (2858-9)
FERRETS Morton (2976-3)
GERBILS Gudas (3725-1)
GERMAN SHEPHERDS Antesberger (2982-8)
GOLDFISH Ostrow (2975-5)
GUINEA PIGS Bielfeld (2629-2)
HAMSTERS Fritzsche (2422-2)
LONG-HAIRED CATS Müller (2803-1)
LOVEBIRDS Vriends (3726-X)
MICE Bielfeld (2921-6)
MYNAS von Frisch (3688-3)
NONVENOMOUS SNAKES Trutnau (5632-9)
PARAKEETS Wolter (2423-0)
PARROTS Deimer (2630-6)
PONIES Kraupa-Tuskany (2856-2)
POODLES Ullmann & Ullmann (2812-0)
RABBITS Fritzsche (2615-2)
SNAKES Griehl (2813-9)
SPANIELS Ullmann & Ullmann (2424-9)
TROPICAL FISH Braemer & Scheumann (2686-1)
TURTLES Wilkie (2631-4)
ZEBRA FINCHES Martin (3497-X)

## NEW PET HANDBOOKS

Colorful and comprehensive guides with
profiles on all major breeds. 144 pages, paper.
NEW AQUARIUM HANDBOOK Scheurmann (3682-4)
NEW CAT HANDBOOK Müller (2922-4)
NEW DOG HANDBOOK Ullmann (2857-0)
NEW FINCH HANDBOOK Koepff (2859-7)
NEW PARAKEET HANDBOOK Birmelin & Wolter (2985-2)
NEW PARROT HANDBOOK Lantermann (3729-4)

## CAT FANCIER'S SERIES

Authoritative books for the serious
owner. Color photos. Hardcover.
BURMESE CATS Swift (2925-9)
LONGHAIR CATS Pond (2923-3)
SIAMESE CATS Dunnill (2924-0)

## NEW PREMIUM SERIES

Complete reference sources. Heavily illustrated,
lavishly produced. Hardcover.
AQUARIUM FISH SURVIVAL MANUAL Ward (5686-8)
CAT CARE MANUAL Viner (5765-1)
DOG CARE MANUAL Alderton (5764-3)
GOLDFISH AND ORNAMENTAL CARP
  Penzes & Tolg (5634-5)
LABYRINTH FISH Pinter (5635-3)

Order from your favorite
book or pet store

**BARRON'S**